What people are saying about *Bridges Of Trust...*

David's works have meant a tremendous amount to me, both professionally and personally, as I manage my way through life as a father, husband, and leader in one of the most incredible and diverse industries imaginable. I recommend David's books to anyone who believes they are a student of life. I enjoyed *Simple Living in a Complex World* immensely, and I am looking forward to reading his and Jim's latest offering, *Bridges Of Trust: Making Accountability Authentic*.

—**Sean Durfy**
President and CEO, WestJet

Bridges Of Trust: Making Accountability Authentic is a powerful and practical guide to learn how to live an authentic life. Many of the concepts are relevant to my role as a president and as a father. I would recommend this book to anyone seeking to make a difference in the lives of those around them.

—**Paul Finkbeiner**
President, Great-West Life Realty Advisors

The authors offer a fresh, inspirational and effective approach to the challenge of accountability, recognizing its importance as a foundation for great leadership.

—**Robin Gerber**
Author of *Leadership the Eleanor Roosevelt Way*
and *Barbie and Ruth: The Story of the World's Most
Famous Doll and the Woman Who Created Her*

You can do all you want about team building and training in an organization, but accountability and authenticity can start only with the individual. An individual's values and identity need to be in sync with the values of the organization. This is David's strength—helping us reach internal alignment. David speaks to business, but you get the feeling that he is really speaking to society—we need more accountability and authenticity. It is easy to see his personal commitment to these two principles. His message is very simple, almost intuitive, but invaluable in today's world where we often look to somebody else to solve our problems for us. Many of us simultaneously think of accountability and of blame, the negative side. David helps us see that accountability is something to get enthusiastic about. Working with him has helped shape our leaders and impact our culture. This book is a breath of fresh air and a must-read for anyone who wants to be more authentic and more accountable.

—**Ed Rodenburg**
President and CEO, Lilydale Inc.

Accountability is one of today's greatest business issues. Fortunately I have been introduced to David Irvine and have benefited first hand from his remarkable insights into not only how to be accountable, but why. He and his organization embody what it means to be accountable and they have been fantastic to work with. David's work with staff and independent advisors has been warmly received, and has supported positive change.

David believes that accountability is a philosophy for living, and he has made himself accountable to help others understand and embrace this message. Take the first step toward refocusing your own accountability—read the book that is in your hands, then implement its strategies. You and those you care about will be better off for it.

—**Ray Adamson**
National Director, Practice Development, Great-West Life

What a great complement to David and Jim's earlier book, *The Authentic Leader*. The authors brilliantly navigate every reader on a personal journey to authenticity and bring the subject to life through their own personal stories. If you're looking to inspire greatness in others that will lead to deep change in your organization—or in your life—then this is a must-read.

—**Durand H. Crosby**
Chief Operating Officer, Oklahoma Department of
Mental Health and Substance Abuse Services

I have been involved with David for more than five years. In my professional role as a senior leader, I worked with him on the application of his two earlier books on accountability and authenticity with my leadership team. His latest book links these aspects together in a new and exciting way. With the current challenges around leadership, the book provides a major roadmap for leaders everywhere.

—**David Stuart**
Senior Director, Environment, Health,
Safety and Security, Petro-Canada (retired)

Our employee team and the store owners who attended the retreat with David are still talking about his presentation and the impact it has had on their lives. David's message of Authentic Accountability continues to provide sustenance and encouragement for myself, my senior team and, most importantly, for our store owners. The ideas shared with all of us are helping us navigate the corridor we find ourselves in with persistence and optimism. David is truly a friend of the Pharmasave family.

—**Doug Sherman**
CEO, Pharmasave Drugs (Ontario) Ltd.

Do you desire contentment, peace, satisfaction and success? Read *Bridges Of Trust: Making Accountability Authentic*. David and Jim clearly show that a better life begins with becoming a better person. They give us tools and ideas to grow as individuals and to create the future we desire.

—**Don Campbell**
President, B-C Ranch Inc., Certified Educator
with Holistic Management International

Bridges Of Trust: Making Accountability Authentic **captures the essence of David's work and makes it applicable in organizations and in everyday life. As a society we have been inundated with material that drives individual rewards and accomplishments. As a coach of sports and management teams, one of the areas I have struggled with is how to form teams from individuals. When a group builds a web of accountability, the collective organization seems to multiply the strengths and minimize the weaknesses.**

Give this book to your co-workers, your employees, your spouse and kids, your kids' teachers and coaches. They will learn, they will change, and they will accomplish more than they ever imagined.

—**John P. Liston, CFP, CLU, CH.F.C.**
Regional Director, The Resource Centre, Great-West Life

Many years ago I attended my first session with David—a presentation with significant personal impact—and many similar opportunities followed. He influences the organizations I lead through my own actions as well as through his sharing at facilitated internal team events. David respects an individual's journey without judgment, while helping others to be authentic and accountable. His presence is real; he walks the talk. Professional development books are steadily populating the store shelves to challenge leaders to maximize their impact; I would rank David's contribution in the top one per cent of material as a must-read.

—**D.A. (Dale) Kelly, P.Ag.**
VP, Agriculture, Biotechnology and Food, Saskatchewan Research Council

Bridges Of Trust: Making Accountability Authentic **will touch your heart and make you dig deep. You'll reflect, learn and never be the same again. Its lessons will inspire and ultimately impact your life in the most positive ways imaginable!**

—**Roberta Kelly**
Executive Director, Credit Union Insurance Services Association [CUISA]

As partners of the Calgary-based architectural firm Marshall Tittemore Architects, we began our accountability process with David Irvine in 2006. By then our firm had grown from only seven individuals to more than 40 in two cities—and a new means of creating alignment among our professional team was required. The existing 'job-description/employee performance' models were no longer effective, especially amongst the firm's senior design, technical and administrative team members.

Accountability agreements now exist between the firm's partners, our directors, team leaders and project managers, and are reviewed at least once per year on employees' employment anniversaries. The accountability process has, without question, been wholeheartedly and enthusiastically endorsed by the participants. It has led to a higher degree of respect between them relative to their individual and collective business goals within Marshall Tittemore Architects.

David's calm, clear, intelligent and inspiring direction was key to garnering the necessary interest and support by the firm's many participants. His ability to relay the personal foundations of his commitment to the accountability process, coupled with the comprehensive, yet straightforward methodology associated with accountability, has led to each one of us enhancing our engagement with the business and profession of architecture.

We now have clearer goals and success measures as well as more meaningful discussions on consequences (i.e. compensation). MTA is now filled with greater purpose at all levels of our firm's activities; we have a more integrated group of leaders in a highly creative and competitive business environment. For that we thank David Irvine.

—**Bill Marshall and Tom Tittemore**
Marshall Tittemore Architects

David is a leader's leader. His writing and teachings have made a difference in my family's life, and have transformed 'accountability' in our organization from a dirty word into a foundational concept.

The authors' perspectives on accountability are profound, and their practice of it transforming. The accountability to each reader is readily apparent from the way the information is organized, to the inclusion of simple lists and tools for making accountability a liberating force in the lives of everyone who embraces them.

—**Jim Ward**
Founder, iomer internet solutions inc.,
Entrepreneurs Organization Forum Moderator

In their new book, *Bridges Of Trust: Making Accountability Authentic*, David Irvine and Jim Reger present each of us with the challenge and the opportunity to move the concept of accountability from an espoused 'value on the wall' to a living 'value in use' in all aspects of our personal and professional lives. I believe this is one of the greatest needs we have today, both in organizations and in society, if we are truly going to make a difference in the world.

As a leader of people services in the public service, I am acutely aware of the need and desire that our organization has to build a culture of accountability. We have worked with David Irvine to link our values, one of which is accountability, to the goal of creating workplace wellness. Our executive team was inspired by this work to develop our own individual accountability agreements as leaders, to help us link our attitudes to our actions. This book provides guidance and inspiration and is a valuable resource on our accountability journey.

—**Mary Jefferies**
Leader, People Services, Alberta Environment

This book is a must-read for senior high school, college and university students. It is essential that young adults make accountability their rule, for which they will gain respect and succeed in their lives. Without accountability our society will fail to improve.

—**Grant Johnston**
Royal Canadian Mounted Police (retired)

I am always inspired when reading David's books or hearing him speak, which I have done on several occasions. His latest book with Jim Reger not only inspires but also provides practical steps to leading an accountable life. A valuable read for everyone.

—**Rick Ehlers**
Executive Vice President, Transmission & Distribution, ENMAX Corporation

Every relationship you have, whether it is in your family, at work or where you volunteer, will benefit when you read and implement the tools in this book. Your work and your results will improve and you will see a difference in how people respond to you. You will be the one people look to for leadership. Having learned from their clients, David and Jim have come up with a blueprint to help others. Years later, people still refer to things they learned in David's sessions as best practices.

—**Robert Sawka**
Director Operations, Pacific Region, Canada Post Corporation

I was the Chief Executive Officer of a growing, profitable retail organization before reading *Accountability, Getting a Grip on Results*. Through implementing the easy to understand steps, and with the assistance of my management team leaders and of David Irvine and Jim Reger, it became extremely clear that my abilities and strengths were unfocused. My time was torn between every department in my organization; I started many different projects, but did not complete each one to the best of my ability. My understanding of what my higher purpose was, what I contributed to the organization, what my personal and corporate goals were, who would help me achieve these goals, how we measure the goals, and to whom I was accountable, was unclear and unstated. Through this process I realized that my role in the organization and how I could contribute the most to its success, was not aligned.

I am now the Chief Financial Officer, I know what my higher purpose is, I know what I contribute to the organization, I know what I am accountable for, I know what supports I need, I know what our goals are and how we measure these goals, and I know what the consequences are whether or not we achieve these goals.

I am less stressed, have a great work/life balance, enjoy my career more and contribute to the organization more effectively and with more energy. The company is growing faster, profitability is up, and my mind is focused, as is my management team. This is not just a great read, but an extremely effective way to create focus and understanding for yourself, your team and your organization.

—**Dale Palmer C.A.**
CFO, La-Z-Boy Furniture Galleries and Kincaid Home Furnishings

In reading *Bridges Of Trust: Making Accountability Authentic*, David and Jim have transformed the word 'accountability.' Often the word has been associated with the responsibility to 'get things done,' sometimes in a threatening and enforcing manner. When we hear the word 'accountability,' sometimes fear, anxiety and pressure emerge! David and Jim's work addresses the essential essence of transformational leadership ... turning accountability from a negative to a positive, moving from an external sense of responsibility to an internal commitment, both professionally and personally.

This book will provide you with specific characteristics and processes to guide you in your personal transformation, enhancing your organization through the distributed leadership model, where the focus is on positive accountability and responsibility for all. It promises a positive working/living environment, success, and positive control.

—**Mary Michailides**
Junior High School Principal

BRIDGES OF
TRUST
Making Accountability
Authentic

by
David Irvine and Jim Reger

D C

PRESS

A Division of the Diogenes Consortium
SANFORD · FLORIDA

David Irvine
156 Toki Road
Cochrane, Alberta, Canada T4C 2A2
Email: david@davidirvine.com
Website: www.davidirvine.com
www.newportinstitute.com

Jim Reger
The Reger Group
110-2659 Douglas Street
Victoria, British Columbia, Canada V8T 4M3
Email: jim@regergroup.com
Website: www.regergroup.com
www.newportinstitute.com

Published by DC Press
2445 River Tree Circle
Sanford, FL 32771
http://www.focusonethics.com

For orders other than individual consumers, DC Press grants discounts on purchases of 10 or more copies of single titles for bulk use, special markets, or premium use. For further details, contact:
Special Sales — DC Press
2445 River Tree Circle, Sanford, FL 32771
TEL: 866-602-1476

Book set in: Adobe Minion Pro
Cover Design and Composition by Jonathan Pennell

Library of Congress Catalog Number: 2009925447
    Irvine. David, and Reger. Jim
Bridges Of Trust: Making Accountability Authentic
    ISBN: 978-1-932021-43-1

First DC Press Edition
10 9 8 7 6 5 4 3 2 1
Printed in the United States of America

To Joan and Val
Who make it all possible

CONTENTS

ACKNOWLEDGEMENTS

There are numerous people whom we particularly want to thank for helping to bring this book to life: Rosemary Cannon, Bernadette Greene, Julia Menard, George DeLure, Bruce Dyck, Bernie Novokowsky, Murray Hiebert, Mel Blitzer, Mary Jefferies, Sarah Phelps, and David Knudson, who took an enormous amount of time to read an early draft of this manuscript and give us such valuable feedback. The book is better because of your perspectives.

Laurie Peck: you helped us get to the heart of this project, and pushed us to bring stories into our theory.

Bruce Klatt and Shaun Murphy, David's original colleagues in this work: you helped to make this philosophy of accountability useful to organizations.

George Campbell: you have been a huge contributor to our thinking about accountability inside organizations.

Susan Levin, our longtime friend and editor: you brought clear thinking, some great stories, and magic to this book.

Our spouses, Joan and Val: without your support, our dreams would never be lived. And our children, Brayden, Natasha, Mellissa, Hayley, and Chandra: you are our consummate lifelong teachers.

We would also like to thank the thousands of participants in our leadership and personal development programs over the years, whose responses to our teaching have been pivotal in helping to formulate our thinking about authentic accountability and its power to transform organizations and lives.

INTRODUCTION TO ACCOUNTABILITY:
A NEW APPROACH TO AN OLD CONCEPT

What if ...

In your organization:

➤ You were building a culture that attracted, retained, and unleashed greatness, where personal and organizational potential was realized?

➤ You didn't have to motivate people, because everyone thought and behaved like *owners*?

➤ The focus was on honesty, communication, and teamwork rather than control and manipulation?

➤ You successfully engaged a workforce that crossed multiple generations?

In your life:

➤ You were clear about your values and priorities, and lived with more inner peace?

➤ Everyone with whom you interacted accepted responsibility?

➤ Blaming was seen as a waste of time?

➤ You didn't have to constantly fight with your children to get them to be responsible?

These questions get to the heart of what it means to be accountable. Everybody's saying it: "Leaders need to be more accountable." "Employees need to be more accountable." "Organizations need to be more accountable." "Kids need to be more accountable." "The world needs more accountability." Yet most accountability programs fail. Why? Because we talk about accountability as if we understand what we are talking about, and we don't.

Both the concept and experience of accountability need rejuvenation. We need to be clear about what accountability *means*, about *who* we are accountable to, and about *what* exactly we are accountable for. Then we need to do what we say we will do, and stand behind our agreements. If these key components are not understood and implemented, accountability becomes just another organizational buzzword, or worse, a hammer to punish people. Accountability is not a program. It is a philosophy for living.

Accountability lies at the foundation of both labor and life. In this book we offer an inspirational and thought-provoking message that will renew your organization, your work, and yourself—whether you work in a multinational corporation, a small entrepreneurial venture, a public service agency, a community association, a health care or educational organization, or whether you simply want to apply these principles to your family. We will show you, through a proven and practical method, how to build an accountability philosophy that sustains focused commitment, transforms organizational culture, and delivers sustained results. Our approach to accountability unleashes human potential, builds trust, and engages people in realizing their true priorities and surmounting their greatest challenges.

WHY WE WROTE THIS BOOK

We have dedicated our lives and our work to inspiring and guiding leaders—in all capacities—to authentically connect with themselves and those they serve, so that they may amplify their impact in the world, and in the process, find meaning and significance in their lives, thus unleashing greatness. Whether you are a CEO, senior executive or middle manager, administrative assistant, frontline service provider or salesperson, parent, artist, schoolteacher, nurse, or community volunteer, opportunities are always available to discover your authentic voice and inspire others to find theirs—in other words, to become an authentic leader.[1] Authentic leadership goes beyond results and getting the job done to making a

---

[1] We discuss authentic leadership extensively in our 2006 book, *The Authentic Leader: It's About PRESENCE, Not Position.* Sanford, FL: DC Press, 2006.

lasting difference in the lives of those you serve. What we found, in our research with hundreds of people over the years, is that people will follow you as a leader if they know that they are dealing with the real you. While some may try to take advantage of your vulnerabilities, you will gain more followers who will admire your courage when you admit you don't have all the answers, and when you support people to find their own path while meeting the needs of the organization.

Authentic leadership and accountability are connected. In order to build a sustaining culture and have a positive impact on the lives of others, you yourself need to be accountable. Leadership begins with taking initiative, and with being dependable, reliable, and trustworthy. Keeping promises—to yourself and to others—builds the integrity that lies at the foundation of an accountable culture.

Accountability also underlies the discovery and expression of your authentic voice in the world. Living accountably means your actions match your core values; you consistently demonstrate self-honesty in a life that is true to yourself.

When you engage in the struggle to be accountable, you are forced to find what you truly value and believe. You begin to live honestly, in harmony with your authentic self, and, in the process, you will be building *bridges of trust, making accountability authentic.* We wrote this book because living accountably is the keystone of our work and of living an integrated life, one that is aligned with the authentic self.

In reading and practicing the principles outlined in this book, you will come to understand a link between authenticity and accountability that will apply to every area of your life. Accountability is where authenticity begins. Facing those qualities which threaten your ability to keep your promises—qualities which are usually rooted in some sort of fear—will reveal to you the barriers between who you are right now, and who you can and will be if you fulfill your potential as an accountable human being. Understanding and implementing a practical approach to personal and authentic accountability will have a positive impact on all aspects of your organization, your community, your family, and your life.

HOW TO USE THIS BOOK

As you read this book, we challenge you to hear the word accountability as if you are hearing it for the first time. We have all been inundated with rhetoric in the flood of management fads. Our commitment is to resurrect accountability from the scepticism and fear that surround it, and show how, with a renewed perspective, it can be life changing.

In addition, we invite you to approach this book in a way that serves you. Rather than reading it front to back, you may want to review the table of contents and start with the chapters most relevant to your situation, needs, and areas of challenge. We suggest you reflect on where you are committed to making a difference in your work as a leader and what your own learning needs are. For example, if you are a frontline service provider in a large bureaucracy, or if you are living in a relationship with someone on whom you cannot depend, then you will find value in the chapter "Dealing with Unaccountable People." If you are a parent or caregiver and are committed to passing on strong values to your children, you will get the most out of the chapter on "Developing Accountable Young People." If you are a leader of an organization wanting to improve a performance management system and you are looking for ways to make existing processes more authentic, powerful, and meaningful, you will find the chapter on "Authentic Accountability Agreements™" helpful. If you want to get clear about your priorities and start living an authentic life that is aligned with your own values, turn to the chapter, "Accountability in Your Daily Life."

No matter which chapter you start with, if you are committed to experiencing the positive results in your life that come from living with greater accountability, we are sure you will find the material useful. As we offer our experiences and perspective, we invite you to bring your own ideas into the experience.

Finally, we welcome your feedback as to how our perspective may have given you some inspiration and support. It is through renewed and stimulating conversations that we keep learning. If you wish to communicate with us, you will find our contact information in the back of the book, or refer to our website at http://www.newportinstitute.com.

CHAPTER 1

OUR APPROACH
TWELVE TENETS ABOUT AUTHENTIC ACCOUNTABILITY

IN THE WORDS OF THE PHILOSOPHER, Henry David Thoreau, *"There are a thousand hacking at the branches ... to one who is striking at the root."* In our view, the following 12 statements strike at the root of accountability. In this book, we hope to reveal the life-changing power that accountability—particularly when it is authentic—can have in your work and in every area of your life. The following fundamental tenets (principles and beliefs) underlie our approach to accountable leading and living.

TWELVE TENETS ABOUT AUTHENTIC ACCOUNTABILITY: IN BRIEF

Tenet One. Accountability is the ability to be counted on.

Tenet Two. Accountability is not about perfection; it's about ownership.

Tenet Three. Authentic accountability is about making promises that are aligned with your values.

Tenet Four. Accountability, when understood and practiced, is energizing.

Tenet Five. There is no such thing as an accountable organization; there are only accountable people.

Tenet Six.	Accountability includes responsibility.
Tenet Seven.	Accountability agreements don't make people accountable.
Tenet Eight.	Accountability is learned.
Tenet Nine.	The best way to build an accountable culture is to hire accountable people.
Tenet Ten.	It's easier to see a lack of accountability in others than to see it in ourselves.
Tenet Eleven.	Accountable leadership starts with you.
Tenet Twelve.	Accountability is about service.

TWELVE TENETS ABOUT AUTHENTIC ACCOUNTABILITY: DISCUSSION

TENET ONE. Accountability is the ability to be counted on.

It is as simple as that. You do what you say you are going to do, when you say you are going to do it, no matter what. You make a promise, and then you honor that promise. You follow through on what you said you would do—regardless of whether it's easy or comfortable—because you said you would. Accountability is more than working hard, being busy, or doing your best. It is delivering the result that you promised. It's carrying through to completion the responsibilities entrusted to you. It's standing up for your actions and for the results of your actions. Whether it's reaching a sales quota, delivering a proposal on time, keeping within a budget, or showing up for a child's soccer game, accountable people keep their agreements. It is for this reason that accountable people think carefully, even if briefly, before making a commitment. They don't make promises lightly, because they know that making an agreement means they'll follow through—regardless of circumstances that may arise. In so doing, accountable people exhibit integrity and inspire trust.

TENET TWO. Accountability is not about perfection; it's about ownership.

Living accountably does not mean you'll never break a promise. Accountable people are, after all, still human. But they take ownership for every agreement they make. For example, when accountable people are late, they don't make excuses. They don't blame the traffic. They simply 'fess up,' take responsibility for being late, and apologize. Most importantly, they learn from the experience and leave earlier next time. Accountable people view all blame as a waste of time. They own their part of the problem, and become part of the solution.

We once met a CEO who was hired to clean up a company on the verge of bankruptcy. Many people in the company chose to blame others rather than take responsibility for their own mistakes. In other words, they weren't accountable. His approach? He began by taking ownership for everything. He didn't blame the unaccountable people. He simply took responsibility for every mistake that was made in the entire organization. Before long, he found people arguing that it was not his problem; it was theirs. The company turned around and is now thriving. Like accountability, ownership is contagious, whether you are a CEO or a frontline service provider. It inspires others to follow suit. We have never met anyone, in all our years of working in and with organizations, who ever thought less of someone who put up their hand and said, "I'm responsible for that."

TENET THREE. Authentic accountability is about making promises that are aligned with your values.

In order for accountability to be authentic, you must first and foremost be accountable to yourself. Authentic people do not compromise their personal principles in order to please others. They stand on firmer ground than popularity or approval. Authentic people are dedicated to seeking, discerning, and moving toward the truth about themselves and bringing this truth—in the form of living their values—into the promises they make. In our society, we tend to yield far too quickly to what is easy and popular, and in the process we give up the pursuit of what is in our hearts. If your promises do not serve both yourself and others, then relationships—at work or in your personal life—will simply not hold any degree of sustained satisfaction. You cannot be true to others if you are not true to your personal core values.

TENET FOUR. Accountability, when understood and practiced, is energizing.

For many, accountability conjures up images of blame, punishment, and fear, all of which drain energy rather than inspire. Our approach to accountability is quite different. Accountability, when it is authentic, is uplifting, energizing, and inspirational. It is invigorating when you are around dependable people who are living their values, people you can trust. Unaccountable people deplete relationships and organizations, whereas accountable people energize their own lives and the lives of people with whom they associate. If you want more energy in your life and in your relationships, then resist the inclination to blame others. Instead, start by taking a careful inventory of where you need to do a better job of keeping your promises—to yourself and others.

There are enormous benefits to living an accountable life. Relentlessly honoring the promises you make to yourself and to the people in your life—colleagues, customers, friends, and family members—will impact your level of self-respect and well-being, the quality of your life, and your success in the marketplace. You fuel your own confidence when you follow through on a commitment in the face of discomfort, inconvenience, and a lack of accountability around you. Also, when you think carefully before making a promise, you learn to say no to the wrong opportunities, and discover how to manage the demands on your time with greater clarity and courage, thus living with less stress.

TENET FIVE. There is no such thing as an accountable organization; there are only accountable people.

We are passionate about building accountable, authentic organizational cultures where trust and respect flourish and where great people choose to come and stay. The way to get there is through personal accountability (within yourself) and interpersonal accountability (between you and others). We know that an organization is only as accountable as the people in it. There will be no accountability in your culture if the individuals who make up that culture are not accountable. People like to blame committees, organizations, governments, or other groups, but in truth, it is the people who comprise those entities who are accountable.

The accountability approach that we outline in this book is not a program imposed by others. It is an individual journey that starts on the inside. Accountability does not require anyone's permission, and does not need to be instituted from the top. Accountability is a personal choice.

TENET SIX. Accountability includes responsibility.

In all our work, the question invariably arises: What is the difference between accountability and responsibility? In theory, accountability addresses ownership, while responsibility refers to execution. You can delegate responsibility; you cannot delegate accountability. For example, if you are accountable for customer service in a department or organization, you can delegate the responsibility to take care of a customer, but if the customer is not satisfied, you, the manager, are the one who is answerable. You can't blame anyone. You may not have trained or supported your customer service representative, or have the right person in the position, but that is the agreement you made in taking on the position.

Asserting this theoretical difference between these two concepts, however, may imply that only managers are accountable, whereas individual contributors are responsible. We feel it is wrong to create two such classes of employees in an organization, with the implication that accountability is the sole domain of management. Because accountability includes responsibility—you can't have one without the other—you will find the two words used synonymously in this book.

TENET SEVEN. Accountability agreements don't make people accountable.

We devote an entire chapter to helping you write Authentic Accountability Agreements™, what we call the new workplace covenant. But don't think for a minute that these agreements are what builds accountability in an organization, any more than a prenuptial agreement makes for a good marriage. An agreement can help to facilitate accountability, but it is not accountability itself. In the book, *Accountability: Getting a Grip on Results* (written by Bruce Klatt, Shaun Murphy, and David Irvine), we focused on developing, writing, and implementing accountability agreements for organizations. In the 10-plus years since the first edition was published, we have learned that these agreements really do work, and that companies and their members who implement accountability agreements seem to work more effectively as a result of the structure they provide.

Taking agreements out of your head and putting them down on paper frees up your creative energy to focus on the work at hand, instead of worrying about what you have promised. The accountability agreements are a great tool for building relationships, getting a grip on results, and aligning strategy with passion in a visible way. They are also very useful tools when teaching accountability to individuals, and we recommend them highly when working with young people or others who have not yet learned how to be accountable.

While there is a time and place for these kinds of formal written agreements, they have their limits. Such agreements, however powerful they are, can't make anyone accountable. They are merely instruments for fostering accountability when the individuals involved are already committed to developing and expressing this quality. A written agreement falls short when it is the sole vehicle for creating accountability, and contracts alone cannot transform a group of people into an accountable culture.

In this book, we offer you insights and tools for creating personal and interpersonal accountability that go beyond accountability agreements. Our approach will enable you to create a culture where it is easier and more rewarding to be accountable than unaccountable, even without formal agreements.

TENET EIGHT. Accountability is learned.

No one is born accountable. It's an attitude and skill you must develop over time. It's best if the seeds of accountability are planted in your early upbringing before you start your career. If people haven't learned to be accountable before they come to work, it's very difficult, but not impossible, to learn once they get there. We feel so strongly about the importance of the influence of the home environment that we have devoted an entire chapter to raising accountable young people.

Regardless of your upbringing, however, you will continue to learn about accountability throughout your life. In many organizations we have seen how individuals at all levels undermine accountability, and people learn by example to be unaccountable. You've no doubt seen unaccountable behaviors in your own organization at times, or even now (it may even be why you chose to pick up this book). Such behaviors lead to a culture where the status quo is to:

- ➤ tolerate mediocrity, where it becomes obvious that goal setting is nothing more than a meaningless paper exercise, where exceptional performance rarely exceeds rewards for the ordinary;
- ➤ reward people for not producing results;
- ➤ enable people to perform badly by not having the courage to follow through on consequences;
- ➤ cover up or ignore unethical, abusive, and destructive behavior.

As you read this book, you will discover how leaders, regardless of their position, can challenge these trends and have a significant influence on the development of accountable people. Through the power of your actions, you can create an environment—in your workplace, in your community, and in your homes—where people can learn to be accountable.

TENET NINE. The best way to build an accountable culture is to hire accountable people.

Because accountability is learned, if you don't learn it when you are young, it is unlikely that you will be accountable as an adult. Therefore, the most effective way to create and sustain an accountable culture in your workplace is to identify people who are already demonstrably accountable, rather than expecting them to have it as part of their philosophy. In your hiring process, explore and assess, at length, whether or not accountability is evident in the candidate's personal philosophy and approach to life. Determine the applicant's values and priorities before you decide to hire him or her.

Here are some practical ways to assess accountability in the hiring process:

Ask potential employees about an experience in their past that would demonstrate accountability. Ask them how they define accountability. Ask them what their values are, and how they display those values in their life and work. Talk with them about their upbringing, about how they learned to be accountable, about how the influential adults in their life fostered accountability within them. Ask them to tell you about a time when they weren't accountable, and what they learned from the experience. When were they challenged to keep their word, to honor their promises, and to show initiative? Be very intentional in the hiring process about assessing whether candidates will bring an accountable mindset with them to work, and whether their values are in accord with the values of the culture you are committed to build.

You'll face an uphill battle if you are dealing with people at a low level of accountability, especially if accompanied by a low level of commitment. If you are a positional leader who is accountable for the culture of your organization, and if you are not deliberately assessing the character of your employees with respect to their level of accountability, your unaccountable employees—whether they are a minority or not—will consume the majority of your energy and time. If this is your reality, at least start by focusing on the people you can count on.

In order to build an organization with a strong commitment to living by a powerful set of core values, it is vital to have clarity regarding what those values are; everyone involved in selecting people for the organization must determine if newcomers already share these values.

TENET TEN. It's easier to see a lack of accountability in others than to see it in ourselves.

When someone else is late, it is easy to focus on their lack of accountability, and even respond with self-righteousness. But when we are the late ones, we often justify our actions. Moreover, not only is it easier to see a lack of accountability in others, it is also easier to talk about accountability than it is to be accountable. All of us slip from time to time.

We encourage you to resist the human tendency to find fault in all the unaccountable people around you. Instead of blaming others, challenge yourself to look inside and take the higher road of ownership. Look for ways you can be more accountable as a person, and track the results in your own life that come from doing so.

DAVID'S STORY: RECOGNIZING THE TENDENCY TO BLAME

When Val, the bookkeeper for the business, discovered that I used a check out of our US account to pay a Canadian invoice, and asked me why I wrote a check that was from the wrong account, my immediate response was to become defensive, rather than to take responsibility and be accountable. My exact words were, "You put the checks in the wrong place!" We all need to avoid self-righteous preaching, and instead frequently remind ourselves that we are no experts in living accountably all the time either—just fellow travelers on the journey.

TENET ELEVEN. Accountable Leadership starts with you.

You'll hear us talk a lot about leadership in this book because it is so central to our work. Leadership is about presence, not position. Leadership is a decision. By choosing to read this book, you have made the decision to be a leader, and to try to make the world a better place because of your presence. Leaders can be found anywhere in an organization, at every level and in any department. Leaders are defined by their actions, not by their titles or the size of their offices. You can be told, "you are now a boss and are in charge of people," but leadership is something you have to earn—in every meeting, in every conversation, and in every decision. If you have made the decision to focus on accountability in your organization, to whatever extent your sphere of influence allows you to, then you are a leader. You can change your organization and the world in which you live by changing yourself. Although you will have less influence at the bottom of the hierarchy than if you are the CEO, you can still have a positive impact no matter what position you hold. Our hope is that no matter where you are in the organizational structure, and no matter what kind of organization you live or work in, these words will inspire you to see the world differently, and to change the world by changing yourself first. In the words of Albert Einstein, "If you change the way you look at things, the things you look at will change."

TENET TWELVE. Accountability is about service.

Motivational guru, Zig Ziglar, once said, "You can have everything in life you want, if you will just help enough other people get what they want." Accountability is ultimately about contributing to others. It flows from a commitment to bring value to others, to work toward the betterment of the world around you. Authentic accountability is the willingness to be accountable for the well-being of the larger community by choosing service over self-interest.

Accountable leaders also recognize the need to balance accountability to themselves with accountability to those they serve. Like all balancing acts, leading with accountability is a dynamic and ever evolving commitment. Having the courage to live and function in the world with this level of commitment breeds a new type of loyalty and commitment in the workplace, where employees will no longer be loyal to the organization at the expense of themselves. In this day and age, people will no longer tolerate "selling their souls" to the corporation for a gold watch at the end. Loyalty in the new workplace will be a commitment to align organizational demands with personal desires, creating a place where people can live their highest values in the service of others, resulting in long-term success and sustainability for the organization and for its stakeholders.

CHAPTER 2

THE BENEFITS AND QUALITIES —AS WELL AS THE RISKS— OF BEING ACCOUNTABLE

The basic difference between an ordinary person and a warrior is that an ordinary person takes everything as a blessing or a curse, while a warrior takes everything as a challenge.

—Don Juan, Yaqui Shaman

TAKE A FEW MINUTES to participate in a short but meaningful exercise. List the people in your workplace or personal life that you can count on. When these people say they will do something, you know it will be done, regardless of the circumstances. Notice the vitality and energy you experience when you think about these people. You might want to take a moment and call these people to let them know you think of them as accountable people, and that you appreciate their presence in your life or organization. We think you will experience a sense of aliveness during these conversations, as you acknowledge their integrity and the meaning it has in your relationship.

Next, make a list of people in your life who depend on you, and ask *them* to try this exercise. Ask yourself, as you do this, "Have I earned the right be on *their* list?" If someone considers you accountable, consider yourself the recipient of extraordinary respect. Vitality, productivity, and decreased stress result when you work and associate with people who are accountable.

DAVID'S STORY: *A DIFFERENT KIND OF ENDORPHIN*

While growing up I learned a simple but powerful lesson about the relationship between self-respect and accountability that has lasted a lifetime. In high school I had a dream to be an Olympic track athlete. At night, before going to bed, I would promise myself to get up at 5 a.m. to train before doing chores on the farm. Five minutes after my alarm clock went off, my father, who was a Canadian gymnastics champion in his youth, would be in my room sitting on my bed. "Son, if you want to be the kind of person it takes to represent your country at the Olympics, you have to learn to keep a promise to yourself—*whether you feel like it or not.*" He would not leave my room until I got out of bed.

One morning, in mid-January in a Canadian winter, after the alarm went off, I got up and read the thermometer outside my bedroom window: -35F. As I crawled back under the warm covers, my father was, once again, sitting on the side of my bed. "David, if you want to be an Olympian, you are also going to have to declare your independence from the weather. Believe me, after you come back from your run in this cold you'll feel much better about yourself than you do at this moment curled beneath those sheets." He was right. I will never forget the good feelings that resulted from that freezing run—because I kept my promise to myself.

In those days I didn't know a thing about endorphins, the chemicals released in the body during exercise that result in increased energy and a feeling of euphoria. Although exercise-induced endorphins are widely recognized today, I have come to understand a different kind of endorphin: the endorphin of *self-respect.* There is no better contribution to your self-respect and energy than to follow through on a promise you have made to yourself or others—not because you "feel" like it, but because it is the *right* thing to do. Self-esteem, I have learned, is not a prerequisite to a good life. It is, instead, the *result* of right living.

Moreover, when you let someone down, you are the only person who cares about the reason why. Since accountability is the key to building trust in a relationship, a lack of accountability inevitably leads to suspicion, low energy, a lack of openness, and decreased commitment. When you follow through on your commitments, the benefits are tremendous. You can live comfortably with yourself. You can walk with your head held high and can face yourself in the mirror, You sleep better, have more energy and inner peace, get better results in your life, and are a force of attraction in the world, because you have earned *self-respect*. When you are accountable in your life, your self-esteem and self-confidence automatically rise. You no longer require approval and happiness from outside yourself. Contentment comes from inside, and you experience serenity in a way that the external world can never provide.

If you reflect upon a relationship in your life that has gone awry, it has, in all likelihood, broken down because of a lack of accountability—a failure to clarify expectations or to keep a promise. Accountable people have less conflict in their lives and are better able to resolve conflicts that do arise. They are more effective at handling change because they are less dependent on external circumstances for their stability. Their security comes from within. Accountability gives you the tools and self-confidence to make better choices in your life as you constantly transform yourself and evolve toward creating more of what you want in life.

Accountability—the ability to be counted on by others—begins with the willingness to keep a promise to *yourself*.

The kind of energy that results from personal accountability is contagious. A respectful and trusting workplace, family, or community begins with *self*-respect—the foundation of all personal and organizational development. Accountability—your willingness to follow through on what is *right*, rather than what is comfortable—will have a positive impact on your organization, regardless of your positional influence.

A final benefit of accountability is what we call the benefit of "structural integrity." In the field of engineering, engineers are accountable for designing structures capable of handling conditions up to a certain limit. In the engineering world, the margin between safety and disaster is known as "structural integrity." Similarly, as the engineers of our own existence, our choices affect not only our own lives but also the lives of the people who rely on us. Our success as accountable people depends on our *personal* structural integrity.

By making the commitment to stand behind the promises we make, by assuming a position of accountability, we begin designing a life of personal structural integrity, a reliable existence that is capable of withstanding the inevitable demands of being alive. After all, it's not the fierceness of the storm which determines whether we break, but rather the strength of the roots that lie below the surface.

When you make a fundamental decision to become accountable for the actions you take in your life, your life will change forever. You forego, permanently, the attitude of blame. You discover that an accountable life is an easier life, not necessarily in terms of comfort, because life brings pain, but in terms of having a solid foundation to support you in the midst of the pain. When you are accountable, you have yourself to turn to, and that is a great comfort in every life situation.

JIM'S STORY: *LEARNING THE HARD WAY*

I have no specific memory of being told by a parent of the importance of accountability. But I was raised by a mother who believed that your word was the most important thing you had. So, as a child, being responsible and accountable was simply a way of life.

However, I do remember a time when I was not accountable, and the effect it had on me. When I was almost 17, I had a part-time job at a large grocery store, stocking shelves, cashiering, and cleaning up at closing time. My dream in those days was to be a disc jockey, an actor, or some other kind of performer. The store manager had taken a shine to me and assigned me the job of announcing the store specials every 30 to 60 minutes over the store's PA system. I took great pride in my position.

The week that I obtained my driver's license, I made sure that everyone in the store, including the manager, knew how much I wanted to save to buy a car, as I lived with my single mother who did not drive and couldn't afford a car. On Friday night I had a date with a very popular girl from school and I planned to take off right at 9 p.m. (Most evenings I stayed, on my own time, 20 to 30 minutes past closing, to ensure everything was properly cleaned up for the next morning.) The manager approached me shortly after starting work that evening and said, "Jim, I need to work late tonight on some paperwork and I'd like to offer my car to you for your date, for a couple of hours. Why don't you take off sharp at 9 p.m. and be back no later than 11 p.m.?" I was very excited about the impression I would make on my first date with this girl, who had arranged for her girlfriend to join us. I was with two of the most popular girls in the school—and a car!

The problem was that I didn't want to end the evening at the time necessary for me to get back to the store by 11 p.m., as my manager had specified. After all, I reasoned, when would I get an opportunity like this again? Their curfew was 11 p.m., and we used every minute. By the time I arrived at the store, it was 11:20 p.m. and the manager was standing outside the store, with everything locked up, waiting for me. All he said was, "I hope you had a good time." The look of disappointment on his face, which I vividly remember more than 45 years later, said it all. Our relationship, though still cordial, was never the same. Reflecting on this experience after so many years, I have concluded that it was my own guilt and inability to forgive myself that changed the relationship. I had broken my manager's trust, and was more disappointed in myself than he was in me—of that I'm certain.

My manager was upset with me because I had never let him down before, but had I approached him the next day with a sincere apology and a promise never to repeat such behavior, I am sure he would have smiled and said, "No problem Jim. So how'd the date go?" The lesson for me was that accountability is not about perfection, but about a willingness to look at ourselves when we make a mistake, forgive ourselves for it, and recommit to be more accountable in the future.

HOW DO ACCOUNTABLE PEOPLE ACT?

Authentic accountability lies in people's behavior. To begin to understand what it means to be accountable, consider the following points that illustrate accountability in action.

Accountable people are both *careful* and *conscious* about the promises they make.

> O wad some Pow'r the giftie gie us
> To see oursels as ithers see us!
>
> —ROBERT BURNS

DAVID'S STORY: *ACCOUNTABILITY AFFECTS YOUR SUCCESS IN THE MARKETPLACE*

My family and I are engaged in a renovation project where most of the windows in the house need replacing, and we have been getting quotes from suppliers. The owner of one glass company measured all the windows and explained that delivery time would be six weeks. He promised to fax a quote the following day. Three days later, after not hearing from him, we called and left a message on his voicemail. The following day, he returned our message and explained that his sales representative had been out of town and was unable to get him the necessary numbers that he needed to provide us with the estimate. He made no apology for being late on the original quote—only an excuse (blame). At the end of the conversation, he made us another "promise," saying that he would get us a quote within "the next couple of days." A week later, after taking our business elsewhere, we still had not heard back from him.

This window supplier may not have been unethical; he may have been *unconscious*. He was unaware of the impact of his actions on his potential customers. He was not conscious of how not keeping promises affects trust in a relationship, and of how important trust is when dealing in the marketplace. Thus, he did not realize how unaccountable he was. We concluded that if this person couldn't deliver on a simple promise to get a quote to us, we couldn't possibly count on him delivering a quality product on time.

If you are committed to increasing your value in the marketplace and in your life, we recommend you start by becoming conscious of the promises you make and the effect you have on others in the delivery of these promises, no matter how small and insignificant they may seem. The window supplier didn't seem interested in hearing our feedback, and therefore missed an opportunity to gain information that could have improved his business in the future. His company may do well when the economy is booming, but the test of how preferred he is as a supplier will come when the market takes a downturn. If you are committed to being accountable, don't blame the *economy*. Instead, take a close look at your *philosophy*. Remember, it's far better to under-promise and over-deliver, than to create unrealistic expectations and let people down. The only way you can know the difference is to stay conscious.

The following concrete suggestions will increase your level of consciousness about the promises you make:

> Be aware—and ruthlessly honest with yourself—about how punctual you are when arriving at meetings. Know that to some people, being five minutes late for a conference call can significantly affect trust in a relationship. Whether you like it or not, that is reality. Don't run the risk of this happening. Plan your life around getting to meetings on time.

> Pay attention to language—especially your own. The words you use greatly impact your degree of accountability. The statements "I'll *try* to be there," or "I *might* be there," are very different from the statement "I *will* be there." When you are "*trying*" or "*mighting*," you are not committing, and are evading accountability. The clearer your language and understanding, the fewer problems you'll have downstream. As Master Yoda, from the legendary Star Wars series put it, "*Do or do not; there is no try.*"

> Be mindful when you are making a promise, regardless how small, of whether or not you are able, and willing, to keep it. Only make promises you know you will honor.

> When you don't keep a promise, apologize and recommit to the agreement. Because your actions affect others, an acknowledgement of any wrongdoing on your part is vital, both to your own self-respect and to trust in the relationship.

➤ Record any commitments you make in your daily planner, so that your promises are in front of you when you are planning your time.

While acknowledging the importance of consciously making agreements and rigorously keeping promises, you must address what happens if, for any reason, you are unable to do so.

Life happens, and, as we stated previously, accountability is not about perfection; it's about ownership. Once you make a promise, you have a creditor, and accountability is about owning your commitment to honor the agreement. If circumstances prohibit you from fulfilling your promise, let the creditor know—*as soon as you know*—that your commitment is jeopardized. Let's suppose, for example, that you promised a customer that you would deliver a product to him at a certain date and time. Two weeks before your deadline, you get a call from your supplier that production has been held up and there will be a two-week delay in delivering the product to you. Upon hearing this, an accountable salesperson will get on the phone immediately and acknowledge your inability to deliver on your promise.

The correct course to take at this point is to review your understanding of the agreement with your creditor, negotiate to minimize damages, and recommit to a new course of action. Take ownership of the problem, without blaming anybody. By doing so, you are offering a *constructive apology*, which is very different than just saying you are sorry. Also, be sure to learn from the experience so you are wiser the next time you make a commitment. In the future, you will need to think more carefully and create a plan should this kind of delay arise again. If you take the time to learn from every failed promise, you can use agreements as continual learning opportunities.

Accountable leaders take initiative.

> *Initiative is doing the right thing without being told.*
>
> —Victor Hugo

Initiative is a willingness to look around, see what needs doing, and take action to make the world better without waiting for permission or direction. If you *own* something, you take care of it, whereas when you *rent* something, you have a tendency to treat it differently. Initiative is about being willing to go beyond the expectations of others, to be an *owner* rather than a *renter* of your life.

DAVID'S STORY: *INITIATIVE AND HOUSEHOLD CHORES*

Initiative is well illustrated in how a family handles household chores. Ownership of keeping the house clean was always a big area of contention between my wife, Val, and me. Because we've always had a housekeeper, in the past I justified acting as a "renter" for the house, and left others to do the chores. I owned my office, my car, and the garage, but with respect to the rest of the house, I was a renter, so I helped but I didn't own. Sure, I was willing to help on the days between visits from the housekeeper, but I failed to step up, to take the initiative to look for what needed doing before Val had to ask me to help. To practice what I preach (and also to be a positive role model for our daughters), I have learned that being a part of a household means taking ownership for keeping the house clean—without having to be asked or reminded.

The best way to illustrate initiative is to observe the owner of a new company who is committed to success. You don't have to motivate an owner. He or she will go the extra mile to make sure the customer is looked after. The life of the company depends on the customer, and an owner knows that. Employees, on the other hand, don't always feel the same sense of ownership, because their investment is not as meaningful as that of an owner. They don't have as much to lose, nor do they have as much to gain. But employees with initiative have an *ownership mindset*. These are accountable employees, and you will never hear them say, "That's not my job" (implying that "I'm just renting it!"). Such employees take responsibility not only for their own jobs, but for their part in the well-being of the whole organization.

The key to great leadership is to instill this ownership mindset in every employee in your organization. While we will discuss how to do this in future chapters, keep in mind that a positional leader can never *impose* an ownership mindset on an employee. What you can do is *inspire* this attitude around you through the power of example, regardless of your position. If you are a custodian and one day you want to own the company, you had better start with owning the shop floor. If you won't take ownership for the little things, how can you expect advancement to anything bigger?

Accountable people take ownership for their own lives, and view blame as a waste of time.

We have not passed that subtle line between childhood and adulthood until we move from the passive voice to the active voice—that is, until we have stopped saying, 'It got lost,' and say, 'I lost it.'
—SYDNEY HARRIS

Accountable people not only own their part of the problem, they also recognize when they are blaming others and stop themselves from continuing that behavior. They resist the tendency to point a finger, and look at themselves instead. Let's be honest, it's a lot easier to blame others than to muster the courage to take the appropriate action for your part of the problem. But that's what accountable people do, and they get rewarded—if not immediately, then eventually—for doing so.

Unaccountable people deny the fact that they, through their perceptions and their choices, are actually helping create the culture and the leadership that they often enjoy complaining about. Realizing and accepting that you have contributed to the creation of the world around you—and that therefore you can contribute to its transformation—is the ultimate act of accountability.

We also blame ourselves too often. A judgmental or critical attitude, regardless of where it's directed, results in inaction. Accountable people don't blame themselves and wallow in destructive guilt. Rather, they take ownership of their part of the problem. If they are experiencing frustration in a relationship—whether it's with their boss, their spouse, or a customer—they take time to examine some fundamental questions, such as: "What is my role in this situation?" "Am I contributing to the problem and, if so, how?" "How could I be more effective in this circumstance?" "What is this experience, no matter how challenging, here to teach me?" What is the opportunity for me?" Accountable people are committed to moving toward a solution that is within their area of control. Because they focus on aspects of their environment over which they can exercise influence, accountable people find sustained power that comes from within, regardless of the circumstances around them. They understand that circumstances do not determine a person; they reveal a person's capacity for growth and change.

Accountable people are direct in their communication, relentlessly avoid gossip, and are loyal to people in their absence.

If you must speak badly of someone, don't speak it,
but write it—in the sand, at the water's edge, near the waves.

—ANONYMOUS

The diagram below illustrates a triad—Person (a), Person (b), and Person (c), who all have a relationship with each other—in a family, a community, or an organization.

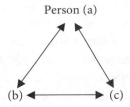

Person (a)

(b) ◄————► (c)

Suppose that Person (b) has a problem with Person (c). An accountable person (b) would either go directly to Person (c) with their problem, or let it go. An unaccountable person (b), on the other hand, would go to Person (a) to complain about Person (c). This kind of gossiping, or backstabbing, signifies a fearful individual who lacks the courage to be direct, or the clarity to let go.

Note that Person (b) may not be the only unaccountable person in this situation. To act accountably in response to Person's (b)'s attempt to gossip, Person (a) needs to be loyal to Person (c). In other words, Person (a) should encourage Person (b) to communicate directly with Person (c) about the issue with the intent of building, rather than destroying, the relationship. If it's appropriate to the relationship, Person (a) may even challenge Person (b) to explore why Person (c)'s behavior has triggered the negative reaction in him or her (i.e., anger, gossip), which may facilitate self-awareness on the part of Person (b).

Building on the positive aspects of the absent party is probably the quickest way to extinguish the destructive fire of gossip. Few things destroy trust, goodwill, and morale in a culture more than backstabbing. Playing any part in gossip—either at the giving or receiving end—leads to an unhealthy culture of indirect communication where scandals and unfounded rumors thrive, and where candor is unappreciated and suppressed. Willingness to communicate directly and let go of resentments, on the other hand, create a foundation for an accountable culture.

Accountable people manage emotions by containing them.

When you are in a bad mood, don't make everyone around you in a bad mood.

—HAYLEY IRVINE, age eight

In his book, *Lessons From The Mouse*, Dennis Snow outlines, from 20 years of experience working at Disney World, 10 lessons on how to create an unparalleled customer experience. His first lesson is *Never Let Backstage Come Onstage*. "Backstage" is behind-the-scenes where cast members eat, drink, complain about management, vent about the previous night's party, and do what anyone on a break would do. Backstage is also designated for truck deliveries, costume changes, composting, company meetings, and so on — things the public is never supposed to see.

"Onstage," by contrast, is where the show takes place. It is everything that happens on each and every stage at Disney World: Main Street USA, at and around Cinderella's Castle, and every other spot you'll find a guest. It's where the customer experience—the "magic"—happens. One of the vital "Lessons From The Mouse" is, emphatically: *Never* let backstage come onstage. Backstage—that mysterious place underground—must be kept "contained," out of sight of the guests.

Every job, every organization, every relationship, has a "backstage," the frustrations, the resentments, the bad moods, the stresses, the personality conflicts, the pain of life. Accountable people are able to keep the backstage "*contained,*" separate from the "onstage" of an organization where productivity, service, trust, and commitment are fostered. Accountable people recognize that while backstage is a part of existence and must be dealt with in constructive ways, it is imperative that backstage does not "contaminate" onstage with negativity. Accountable people have the capacity to deal productively with the backstage, so they can step onstage with a commitment to contribute in both a real and constructive way.

To better understand this notion of "containment," stop and reflect for a moment on the following question: "Is fire good or bad?"

Answer: it depends on whether the fire is *contained*. Fire, contained in a furnace, will heat a building. That same fire, uncontained, has the power to *destroy* the building.

Now reflect for a moment on this question: "Are emotions good or bad?"

Feelings, like fire, are neither "good" nor "bad." Their value depends on whether they are contained. Accountable people have the ability to contain their emotions and manage their personal reactions to situations appropriately. Unaccountable people often lack the courage or discretion to do so.

Emotions such as frustration, anger, fear, and hurt are present in every relationship, organization, or culture. *Containing* such emotions acknowledges feelings by honoring two vital virtues: respect and truthfulness. When you contain your emotions, you first acknowledge to yourself when these feelings arise. Then, you step back and examine the most respectful and truthful way of expressing them. Finally, you take appropriate and positive actions.

Young children, who have yet to learn accountability, do not have the maturity level required to contain their feelings. A frustrated four-year-old is unlikely to stop and contain his or her feelings by first acknowledging them and then assessing the most respectful and truthful way of expressing them. The angst-ridden four-year-old will instead spew out the uncontained emotion in the form of a temper tantrum. You expect this type of destructive behavior from a four-year-old while he or she is learning to be accountable. But it's problematic when a 40-year-old is still contaminating his or her environment with temper tantrums and incessant complaining!

Containing emotions is different than suppressing or sublimating them. Emotions, after all, come and go. Containing means observing your feelings and deciding what you will do with the energy they represent. It means dealing with emotions *intelligently* rather than reacting to them *impulsively*. It may mean dealing directly with people, or it may mean getting support away from the situation so you can let go with dignity. It may also mean exploring what might be a deeper, unacknowledged, and authentic need.

Here are a few practical ways to contain feelings:

> *First*, distinguish between "venting" and "complaining." Venting is appropriate because it is contained. It has a beginning and an ending. It is honest. It is done behind closed doors, in an office or contained place, and is respectful of others who are not

present. Venting is constructive because you share your feelings. Complaining, on the other hand, is inappropriate because it is not contained. It is done in the open, which fuels gossip and negativity. It is destructive because it is critical of people who are not present. It has no end, and poisons a culture.

➤ *Second*, step back from emotional situations before responding. Rather than impulsively reacting to a stressful, frustrating or highly charged emotional situation, step back, at least momentarily, and develop a strategy for responding in a way that is respectful and beneficial to all. This is not the same as withdrawing or denying your own emotions. It is, instead, about waiting to respond until you have an appropriate and constructive action planned. In developing a plan of action, having a confidant— usually away from your situation—to give support and perspective, can be helpful. Alternatively, take the space and time to think through an appropriate plan. Then, whether your plan involves being direct with the people involved or simply letting go, "containing" means you are a force of constructive action that builds rather than diminishes.

➤ *Third*, make time for one-on-one dialogue. Complaining, gossiping, and criticizing are not just symptoms of insecure, immature, unaccountable people, they can also be indicators of a culture that does not support people taking the time to actually talk to each other directly. If you live or work in a place where you hear, "we are too busy to develop relationships or resolve differences directly," then in all likelihood, you will find a culture of complaining. When people don't connect, they complain. Containing feelings means making time, even when you don't "have the time," to build relationships, understand each other's needs and expectations, and resolve differences directly, in the spirit of goodwill and respect.

➤ *Fourth*, stick with the winners. The best way to contain feelings is to hang around people who are the builders in an organization, the accountable leaders that you find at every level of the culture who are committed to greatness. Accountable people have no energy to expend on the whiners, complainers, or those who tear down others. They spend time looking for solutions. They focus on what's going right, and they are committed to making the culture better. Accountable people are positive and constructive, and they spend time in like-minded relationships. A few committed people, who band together for a good cause, can change the world. Indeed, perhaps this is the only way the world has ever changed.

Accountable people let go of the past so it does not hold them back.

At some point in our lives, we are going to have the experience of being betrayed, hurt, or treated unjustly. Just as accountable people step back from their emotions, they also step back from their life experiences in order to learn and grow from them. At times life does not appear to be fair, but if one takes time to examine the whole story, it will eventually balance out, and the good will emerge from the pain and temporary discomfort.[1] The sooner we accept life's setbacks as challenges, the sooner we step into living accountable lives and thereby discover (or recover) our freedom. Instead of reacting by playing the victim, accountable people take time to examine their beliefs, discard those that are outdated and hinder their progress, and learn to treat each setback as a learning experience, thus becoming stronger, more complete, and more competent. If you are finding yourself being robbed by resentment, blame, addiction, or unmanageable fear, we encourage you to take time to deal with your past and take an honest look at yourself. Accountable people, through both courage and support, eventually build a bridge and get over it.

Below is a list of practical ways you can use to let go of the past that may be holding you back:

> ➢ Have the courage to take a thorough personal inventory of yourself—without blame. Be honest with yourself. Acknowledge if you are stuck in a self-destructive pattern that you can't seem to free yourself from (e.g. an addiction, destructive situations, barriers in your career development, problems with anger management, insecurity, or any recurring difficulties in your life).

> ➢ Find a good psychotherapist, mentor, or coach who will guide you to a new perception of yourself by assisting you to acknowl-

---

[1]For a more in-depth understanding of this balance, see David Irvine's *Simple Living in a Complex World: Balancing Life's Achievements* (Canada: Wiley & Sons, 2004), in the chapter titled, *Maybe I Am Fortunate*, 35–41.

edge your past, challenge your limiting beliefs, and help you let go of that which is holding you back.

➤ Twelve-step programs can be extremely valuable in helping you face yourself and find freedom from your past through the process of self-honesty, support, spiritual growth, and accountability.

➤ Read books or sign up for courses that will increase your level of self-awareness, help you let go of the past and enable you to grow by connecting you with your authentic self. Information about our *Intensive Authentic Living* retreats is available at the back of this book or on our web site: www.newportinstitute.com.

➤ Adhering to a spiritual practice of meditation or prayer can be helpful in learning to let go and take responsibility for your life.

Accountable people focus on results; they know that activities and merely keeping busy are not enough.

At the end of each day, you should play back the tapes of your performance. The results should either applaud you or prod you.

—JIM ROHN

Everyone in an organization, from the CEO to the frontline service provider, has some piece of business and a corresponding set of results that is theirs to achieve. If it's your area, function, or project, you are accountable. For an organization to flourish, each member must produce results. Being busy is not enough. Accountability for results is more than simply completing the list of activities in your job description.

Consider a team of firefighters who arrive at your home to extinguish a fire. Simply driving the fire engine, blasting the siren, and guiding the hose with the fire blazing is not enough. Firefighters don't have a job description with a long list of activities. What matters for them are results: *they must put out the fire and save lives—fast.*

Accountable people shift their thinking from activities to results, and in so doing create an awareness of why they do what they do. Accountable people, whether in families, communities, or organizations, ask themselves and others to whom they are accountable, *"For what results am I accountable?"* and *"For what results are you accountable?"* They negotiate these expectations clearly and carefully, and commit to creating those results—without any excuses.

Often we have a "job description mentality," wherein we list the duties (in the form of activities) required of us, rather than the *results* we promise to deliver. Accountable people reframe their job descriptions into the means to achieve results, but understand that those results may require more of them than the duties outlined in their job description. Taking the initiative to own the process necessary to achieve the expected results is foundational in building accountability.

Accountable people are guided by a higher purpose.

Whatever you can do, or dream you can do, begin it. Boldness has genius, power, and magic in it. Begin it now.

—SOURCE UNKNOWN

In *Alice's Adventure in Wonderland*, Alice asks the cat, "Would you tell me please which way I ought to go from here?"

"That depends a good deal on where you want to get to," said the cat.

"I don't much care where ..." replied Alice.

"Then it doesn't matter which way you go," said the cat.

Unlike Alice, accountable people are guided by a sense of purpose and destiny. They have a vision and clear values that give them a framework for decision-making. Because accountable people are not dependent on others for their self-esteem and approval, they are directed by an inner sense of what their life is about. Therefore, they don't depend on others for direction, recognition, or security. They consider the culture around them, but they create their own vision, and hold themselves accountable for creating what matters most to them and what serves the greater whole. They know from experience that personal security lies *within*. They are able, through the energy of their vision, to communicate this vision to others in a way that engages and enlists others. They are clear about their priorities and have understandable processes for putting first things first. Although they may have a to-do list that is in alignment with their planned results, they have clear boundaries about what is "right" and "wrong" for themselves, what they stand for, and where they will and won't go. They also have a *don't-do* list, made up of demands that lie outside their values system or priorities. Their framework for decision-making is clear because they are clear about their values—and they will not compromise those values, regardless of the situation. It can take as much discipline to say no to a wrong opportunity as it takes to fulfill a right one.

There is a story of three bricklayers working side by side. A passerby, aroused by curiosity, asked each of the workmen what they were doing.

In response, the first bricklayer replied, "I'm making mortar."

The second bricklayer said, "I'm laying bricks."

The third bricklayer responded, "I'm building a cathedral."

A higher purpose is what inspires you in your work, lifts you in moments of discouragement, and transforms drudgery into opportunity. Stop for a moment and reflect on the following question: *What causes you to jump out of bed in the morning, eager to face the day?*

A higher purpose motivates you to learn the extra skills, to put in the extra time, to go the extra mile. It inspires you to step out of blame, gossip, and destructive communication because you know that you are on a more important path than that of wallowing in self-pity. If you find yourself stuck in negativity, seek a path of purpose, and hold yourself accountable for living your vision. Pursuing this vision—with all of its attendant risks and sacrifices—will inspire you to become accountable.

Accountable people focus on their passions, not their pension.

Only passions, great passions, can elevate the soul to great things.
—DENIS DIDEROT

An entire generation walked before us and paved the road to our freedom and financial and social stability, enabling us to live our dreams and follow our passions. Our grandparents' generation lived through hard times, went to war, and rebuilt our society. From these brave and dedicated individuals we inherited virtues such as duty, hard work, and loyalty at all cost, as they dedicated their lives to their country, their employers and their loved ones. If we are open to learning about extinguishing undeserved entitlement and self-centeredness, this previous generation can teach us much. They had a tacit understanding of accountability, and this foundation enabled us to evolve into a new kind of world.

The price of this kind of commitment to duty and "loyalty at all cost," however, is that many in this generation would be viewed today as "selling their soul," giving up their authentic self, for the sake of the organization.

We are certainly not against pensions or working hard for a number of years to ensure yourself and those you care about some financial freedom in your older years. It is the focus on pension at the expense of passion that we are concerned about. Instead, we are committed to supporting people to discover a new kind of accountability, an accountability to yourself and those you serve to live life with passion so there are no regrets at the end of your career.

Unlike many of our grandparents, we now have the opportunity for *authentic* accountability. In other words, we have the chance to integrate a commitment to our passion—the deep and abiding voice within that fuels our reason for being, provides an endless supply of creative energy, guides our hearts, and brings meaning to existence—with the needs of the organizations that employ us. This is the new workplace—a place in which we can find both personal *and* financial growth, where we can experience a new kind of loyalty both to ourselves and to the organizations we serve.

Just as accountable people don't live in the past, neither do they live in the future. Accountability ultimately teaches you to live in the present. In this new world accountable people can redefine retirement as a vision for which to prepare by living a full life *now*, not a fantasy to yearn for, thereby wasting today's opportunity for experience. That stage of life can be an opportunity for a new career and a new life with renewed challenges and opportunities, not unlike what they have now. The message is to seek your fulfillment in the *now*, for it is likely that if you are unhappy now, when you "retire," you may well be just as unhappy.

To conclude this segment on purpose and passion, we feel it is important to offer you a note of caution. If you are considering changing your current situation in favor of one that seems to be more aligned with your higher purpose or a passion, before you do so, first commit yourself to be all you can be where you *are*. Serve and learn all you are meant to learn and contribute in your present environment. If you leave prematurely, you'll be certain to meet the same challenges and roadblocks next time around. Once you have given your all, you'll know if and when it is time to exit. The grass is never greener on the other side of the fence. It's greener where you water it!

Accountable people are lifelong learners.

Accountable people are "learners" rather than "knowers." "Learners" are people who do not define themselves by what they know. Their worth is not conditional on being right. Their identity is not static, but is continually changing and growing, so there is always room for new possibilities and growth. Their ego is not attached to being "right." Accountable people are open to lifelong learning. The best leaders are learners, because they take the best from everything they experience and use it to improve their understanding of issues, and therefore see opportunities that knowers would miss.

Accountable people have ethical boundaries.

Accountable people live by a personal code of ethics, defined as:

> ➤ **Core values:** They have clarity about what matters most in their lives, and make these values explicit to the people who depend on them. They understand that ethical breaches begin internally.
> ➤ **Character:** They have clear principles that translate values into action, and hold themselves accountable for doing so. People of strong character are also willing to be held accountable by others whenever there is a lack of congruence (perceived or real) between their stated values and their conduct. People of strong character also live by a commitment to improve the lives of all the constituents they serve.
> ➤ **Clear ethical boundaries:** Ethical people uphold standards of behavior for themselves by living within defined parameters that they do not cross. They understand that true values cannot ever be fully known until you are put in a position of choice, until they are tested under pressure. Ethical people stand on higher ground than popularity, social approval, financial security, or personal comfort. They are internally clear about what is right for themselves, and they make these boundaries clear to the people who depend on them.

RISKS OF ACCOUNTABILITY

While living an accountable life is a powerful way to focus human energy, there are risks. It would be naïve not to highlight at least some of these risks.

You have to be willing to withstand some discomfort and rejection, and stand alone. Just because you are personally accountable, don't expect to win the approval of the masses for your honorable choices. Accountability is not for the faint of heart. It can be both painful and lonely to keep your commitments, no matter what, when you no longer have the "out" of rationalization with which to evade your conscience. Facing the discomfort of standing by your values, principles, and promises amid cultures that are willing to give in to the tides of change, popularity, and greed is a risk that accountable people must be prepared to take. We have experienced rejection from others and have rejected professional opportunities because they were not aligned with our values. Even though it is our experience that accountability builds respect in the marketplace, we don't expect it to lead to public recognition or approval. Yet we have found it is always worth it in the long run, despite the short-term sacrifices.

Being accountable can lead to short-term financial loss. A short time ago, one of our clients told us about a recent transaction he had with a customer, a story familiar to accountable people. He had recently taken an order from a customer along with a deposit for the goods. In return, he had promised the customer a quote and a delivery date one month later. A week after the order was placed, he received a call from his supplier, stating that since the order was taken, the price of the product had increased. Even knowing that the customer had been promised the lower price, the supplier wouldn't budge.

"My first impulse," our client said, "was to call the customer, blame the supplier for both the price increase and his rigidity, and add the increase to the customer's bill. But then I thought about what I had been learning about accountability, especially about taking ownership. I decided this was my problem, not my customer's. To be accountable, I needed to do what was right, not what was easy, so I decided to absorb the increased cost. At one level, this was short-term loss for long-term gain. This customer knows I am accountable from our previous dealings and she will be with me for a lot longer. But, frankly, that's not why I made this decision. At the end of the day, doing what's right—being accountable—enables me to look myself in the mirror at night with some self-respect."

Accountability can lead to over-responsibility and burnout. Often, by taking ownership for everything that happens to you, it is easy to assume more than your share of responsibility in any given situation. There is a definite line, though not always clear, between being accountable *to* others and being accountable *for* others. We are encouraging the former and cautioning you about the latter. Over-responsibility can foster a drive for perfection, an attitude that "no one can do this as well as I can," and a reluctance to delegate. Accountable people must always be on guard for this, ensuring that they set clear boundaries, know where their accountability stops, and know how to let go and say no.

CHAPTER 3

ACCOUNTABILITY IN YOUR DAILY LIFE
PERSONAL LEADERSHIP, HABITS, AND STAYING FOCUSED

You can't build a reputation on what you are going to do.

—HENRY FORD

B Y NOW YOU HAVE LEARNED that accountability can be a sustainable source of energy, self-respect, inner peace, confidence, and the respect of others. All of these are the result when you commit to and follow through on agreements that are in alignment with your values. In addition, accountability is about *action*. The choices you make and the habits you form build your character and determine your destiny.

A big difference exists between knowing something and actually following through with action based on that knowledge. How many people know that exercise is good for them but don't make the time to exercise? How many know that it is essential to spend time with loved ones but don't? How many are trapped in the grips of an addiction but don't do anything about it?

You can't be accountable to others until you are consistently accountable to *yourself*. Accountable living requires that your actions follow your words; in other words, that you be authentic. In this chapter, we offer you a seven-step process for achieving authenticity and accountability in your daily life. Remember, it is not what you feel like doing or say you will do that can change your life, but rather what you actually *do* with your life that will change it.

THE SEVEN STEPS TO ACCOUNTABILITY IN YOUR DAILY LIFE: *IN BRIEF*

Step One.   Decide that blame is a waste of time.

Step Two.   Connect with your authentic self.

Step Three.   Connect with the important people in your life, and make promises accordingly.

Step Four.   Schedule the big rocks first.

Step Five.   Take time for daily reflection.

Step Six.   Practice integrity in each moment.

Step Seven.   Create an authentic community to support you and hold you accountable.

THE SEVEN STEPS TO ACCOUNTABILITY IN YOUR DAILY LIFE: *DISCUSSION*

Sow a thought and you reap an act;
Sow an act and you reap a habit;
Sow a habit and you reap a character;
Sow a character and you reap a destiny.
—William Makepeace Thackeray

STEP ONE. Decide that blame is a waste of time.

Before you can change the world, you must change yourself. All the great teachers instruct that in order to make a change in your life, you must use whatever problems you are facing to look at yourself. If you are suffering, whether in your workplace, a significant relationship, or within yourself, decide to make it your problem, regardless of any others who are involved. As you learn to respond in a new way to everything that happens to you, if you let go of blame toward yourself and others, and look within instead, you will not only empower yourself, you'll actually start a new life.

Here are some examples of people we have worked with in our coaching program who made a decision to stop blaming and start living. They are in no particular order—just "ordinary" people making extraordinary decisions that changed their lives:

> ➤ An alcoholic, spending years of his life owned by booze, finally made a decision to stop blaming everyone around him for his problems and to take responsibility for his recovery. He called a treatment facility, admitted his powerlessness over alcohol, and began his journey home.

> ➤ A woman, who for months was resentful of her boss for her excessive workload and non-supportive work environment, finally made a decision to get on with her life after receiving some very difficult feedback from her subordinates. "After much hard soul-searching, I realized that my negativity in the office was really a mask that covered my fear to change. I am beginning to see that this is a pattern in every area of my life. I am determined to start changing my attitude and actions, and stop complaining about things outside of my control."

> ➤ An underachieving salesman realized that his blaming the economy and the downturn in the markets was just a way to avoid looking at changing the way he was doing his work.

Blaming, with its attendant negativity, judgment, and criticism, is a safe way to avoid facing change and to stay stuck. When you make a decision to stop blaming, you create space for something new to be born. Saying *no* to blaming is like walking away from a toxic relationship in your life. Frightening though it may be, it is ultimately freeing because you are no longer looking outward for others to change so that you can change. Now you can start to change yourself into a better person, regardless of anyone or anything. Your future no longer lies in someone else's hands.

When you focus on yourself rather than on others, you also gain the opportunity to learn about yourself, which in turn leads to the opportunity for you to change. When you are up against a difficult situation or a barrier in any relationship, instead of assigning blame, ask yourself questions such as, "Where have I met this situation before?" "Is there a pattern in my response?"

"What can I learn about myself here?" "Why did this situation come into my life at this time?" "What am I being called to do or be in this situation?" And, "Who might assist me in finding a new perspective and to support me to make a change?" An accountable person will always see difficulty as both a challenge and an opportunity to learn. The difficult people in our lives are often our greatest teachers.

Finally, accountable people do not depend on the approval of others or on expectations as they take the higher road of ownership and learning. They take action because it is the right thing to do. They do not depend on social mirrors for their sense of security or self-esteem; they set their own standards instead. They are always harder on themselves than they are on others. Accountable people live by an unwritten motto: "If it is to be, let it begin with me."

STEP TWO. Connect with your authentic self.[1]

> *One's self is at the base of everything. Every action is a manifestation of the self. A person who doesn't know [him or herself] can do nothing for others.*
> —EIJI YOSHIKAWA, JAPANESE HISTORICAL NOVELIST

As a leader, you spend every day putting out fires. Then one day you look inside yourself and notice that your own fire is out. What happened? In the hurry to make a living, you neglected to make a life.

All too often we find ourselves reacting to the demands of daily life, rather than responding to our authentic desires. Life becomes a little too much like being on a boat where the oarsmen are all pulling in different directions.

These days, most people struggle with managing time. No one who makes meaningful contributions and lives a full life in our society is immune from enormous daily pressure. On some days, life seems to be nothing more than a messy trail of uncompleted to-do lists and unmet responses to a demanding world. The thoughts of unanswered emails, missed opportunities, unvisited friends, abandoned talents, and neglected commitments haunt

---

[1]For those committed to going deeper on the authentic journey, see *Becoming Real: Journey to Authenticity*, by David Irvine, and *The Authentic Leader: It's About PRESENCE, Not Position*, by David Irvine and Jim Reger.

our tranquil moments when we stop to reflect upon our lives. Living in a demanding world, if you are not intentional about it, will pull you away from your authentic self, thus disabling you from being accountable. After all, how can you possibly become an accountable, dependable person—who can sustain this sense of reliability long-term—if you are depleted, burned out and out of touch with what is important to you?

Accountability ensures that you keep your promises. *Authentic* accountability aligns these promises with your core values, that is, with your authentic self. Connection with your authentic self informs you as to your personal needs and desires. Once you have this knowledge, living accountably means protecting your personal needs and desires, rather than allowing those of others in your life to take precedence. With self-awareness, you also avoid the danger of focusing on external success, and instead become the person you are meant to be.

Below is an exercise to help you connect with your authentic self by understanding what your core values and beliefs are and how you formed them.

Our values and beliefs are influenced by the various cultures and communities which we were exposed to over the years—family, neighborhood, school, career, leisure activities, friendships, religion, politics—and the meaning we made out of these experiences. We invite you now to stop and give yourself permission to get away from your usual environment to a place where you can be reflective and creative. The exercise has three parts: a) personal reflection, b) a statement of higher purpose, and c) authentic accountability. The exercise will take two to three hours to complete, and can be life changing if you create the space and invest the time. Resist the human tendency to just read through this section. Commit to a time in the coming week to spend reflecting carefully about the answers to these questions. As with most things in life, you will get out of it what you put into it.

A. Personal Reflection

Begin by dividing your life into what we call the eight life stages, beginning at birth and ending at your present age: zero–five, six–12, 13–21, 22–35, 36–49, 50–63, 64–72, and 73 and beyond. *Be certain to use a separate sheet of paper for each stage,* and answer the following questions in relation to the stage you are examining. Do the best you can with your current memory. Don't get overly concerned with exact ages. This is about getting a general sense of your experiences and the meaning you made of your experiences at each period of your development.

Questions (to be answered separately for each stage of your life):

➤ Describe the *persons* who influenced the development of your character—your values, principles, and beliefs that guide your actions today. These could be actual people in your life (parents, siblings, relatives, coaches, teachers, friends, etc.), heroes (real or imagined) or leaders (living or not). What were the qualities of each person who had an influence on you?

➤ What were the primary *events* that influenced your character? Consider any "defining moments" (events that significantly altered your perceptions or outlook on life, causing you to change in some way—either because you were "forced" to or because you chose to. Examples would be a move, a death, a birth, an illness, etc.) What meaning did you make of these experiences? How have these events influenced you?

➤ What were the primary *values and beliefs* that you developed during this period? How were your primary values helpful to you at that time? How were they not helpful?

➤ What were your *passions and dreams* during this period?

➤ What are you still holding on to from this period? Events? Emotions? People? Is holding on helping or hindering you today?

B. A Statement of Higher Purpose

Many people capture the answers to these questions in a written personal mission statement, vision statement, personal creed, or some form of a values statement. Regardless of what kind of statement you use or what you call it, in order to live an accountable life you need to conceptualize, in a way that is meaningful and unique to you, a higher purpose for yourself beyond your daily to-do lists. It will include what you want to be and do with your life, what you stand for as a person, and the principles that guide your life. Clarity on these issues, as expressed in your statement of higher purpose, is vital for two reasons. First, it becomes an inner compass, a framework for the decisions you make and how you spend your time. Second, it provides a source of inspiration to you in the darker moments of your life when your spirit weakens or when you find yourself discouraged or drifting from your authentic self.

Following are two sample personal Statements of Higher Purpose. Note that their power comes not from having the "right" words, but from the process experienced in clarifying what matters most in the person's life, and in making it concrete by writing it out. The first, Jim's statement, sets forth various lists of values and guidelines. The second, David's, comes in the form of a mission statement and a list of core values to which he is committed.

After you develop your own unique vision statement, we suggest that you take time away from your day-to-day life at least once a year, to review, renew, and revise this document as your life evolves. During this time you may want to set some specific goals in each of the core areas of your life that need attention during the upcoming year. We suggest an annual retreat for some personal reflection time, in surroundings that uplift you and help you to get focused.

You may find other ways of expressing your higher purpose and values besides a vision statement. You may find that segmenting your authentic self into values, mission, vision, principles, or guidelines actually makes your life feel compartmentalized and fragmented. Our examples indicate months of personal reflection and careful thinking about what defines our lives and our values. Find a way to make this meaningful for you. As long as you reserve some time to step away from the frantic pace of your life and do some serious thinking about what matters most to you, it doesn't matter what you call your work in Step Two. The results depend on the sincerity of your commitment to changing your life, and on your honesty with yourself about your values. Self-honesty is critical in this process, because unless the agreements you make in your life are in alignment with your authentic self—i.e., your inner voice of truth—your promises will either burn you out or leave you dissatisfied.

Step Two may take months to develop. Proceed with subsequent steps while you are working on this step, and don't be in a rush. Anything worth doing is worth doing *slowly*. Set aside time—whether it's 30 minutes a day or a couple of hours a week—for some reflection, thinking, and quieting of your mind. You might also find value in keeping a journal to record the thoughts, feelings, and observations that arise from these reflective moments. Writing, whether in a journal or on a notepad, is a great tool for seeing your life in a new light. The discovery of your authentic self is not a destination, but a life-long journey, a method of travel.

JIM'S STATEMENT OF HIGHER PURPOSE:

My Core Values and Beliefs

- I am a spiritual being with free will.
- I have the right to be all I can be and make the most of my life.
- I can create my own beliefs about anything in life. Knowing that I always have this choice empowers me to create my own results.

My Higher Purpose

- To learn, grow, and evolve as I live my life with integrity—being true to my authentic spiritual self.

My Guiding Principles

- To live my life in the present with passion, faith, courage, and honesty.
- To be accountable and responsible for the choices I make, and respectful of the choices others make.

My Professional Guidelines

- To do work that excites me—and not do work that does not excite me.
- To have an attitude of abundance—trusting that there will always be enough (money, love, etc.).
- To give back to society and to the less fortunate.

My Personal Guidelines

- To always let my family know how much I love them—with words and with actions.
- To lighten up and be more fun.
- To expand my circle of close friends.
- To meditate regularly.

DAVID'S MISSION STATEMENT:

I inspire and guide leaders to connect with their authentic self, that they might inspire and guide those they serve to find their true voice, thus unleashing greatness.

I inspire, illuminate, and encourage authenticity in leaders. (If one is committed to serving, to influencing, to making the world a better place through a clearer and stronger expression of one's authentic voice, then one is, by my definition, a leader.)

My life is lived, to the best of my ability, in accordance with my top six values that have unique and personal meaning to me. Below is what I call my "Declaration of Interdependence:"

1. Faith—Faith is trust and reliance upon a higher power, a compassionate force that is moving me, knowingly or unknowingly, toward growth, wholeness, and completeness. It is my creator to whom I am ultimately accountable.

2. Strong Character—Character is the expression of my faith in the world. It reminds me that I am a human *being*, not a human "doing." Character is about the kind of person I am committed to be, thus enabling me to pass the mirror test at the end of the day: when I look at myself in the mirror I have self-respect. Character consists of the following virtues that I hold to be important:

COURAGE—The virtue that precedes all other virtues.

HUMILITY—A true evaluation of conditions as they are, a reliance on a power greater than myself.

HONESTY—A dedication to seek, discern, and move toward the truth about myself and to act in accordance with that emerging awareness; freedom from self-deception, trustworthiness, dependability to keep promises to myself and others; living life without pretence; the strength of vulnerability.

[CONTINUED ON PAGE 42]

PRINCIPLED—Rather than making decisions and taking actions based on the fleeting allure of emotions, or whether the action is necessarily "easy" or "hard," decisions and actions are based on what is right.

EXCELLENCE—Anything worth doing is worth giving it my all.

PRUDENT—The common sense to decide what I can do without.

MATURITY—Claiming responsibility for my life, without blame.

GRACIOUS—Respect and kindness to everyone I interact with.

GRATITUDE—The antidote to all that ails me.

CONTRIBUTION—"To give is to live;" the ongoing commitment to overcome self-centeredness through compassionate service.

GRACEFUL—Open to surprise, being present.

SELF-ACCEPTANCE—Being human is more important than the illusion of perfection.

3. Health—My body is the vessel that carries me and is vital for fulfillment of my destiny. As such, it requires attention and care. Health habits create quality of life; later life will test this. My body is also a barometer of my inner well-being.

4. Marriage and Family—Marriage is the base camp of my life's Mount Everest, a refuge from the challenges of life, and a sanctuary. Family is the ultimate expression of love in my life. My family requires attention and nourishment. Through it I am learning a balance of giving and receiving.

5. Stewardship—I am a steward of the gifts I have been given. As such, my responsibility lies in finding, expressing, and fulfilling these talents in the service of others to the best of my ability. My business, my paid work, is a tool for living this value in my life. My career is an *expression* of myself, rather than a definition of my worth.

6. Community—Community comprises the people in my life with whom I can be completely open and honest, people who support me, people who hold me accountable for living in accordance with my values, and people who care more about my soul than they care about my ego.

C. Authentic Accountability

This part of the exercise is about defining your core values and the power of living your life in accord with those values. Now that you have taken some time to look at your past, take time to consider and then respond to the following questions:

> What are the top five values in your life? What matters to you most—beyond economic and material success? Relationships? A sense of purpose? Peace of mind? Health? Contribution/Service? Personal Character? Achievement?

> Now for each of these core values, create a corresponding personal goal that you can accomplish in the next one to three years. In other words, what areas in your life need attention (e.g., your inner, spiritual life; your unfulfilled dreams, passion or creativity; your relationships; your health; your work; your contribution to others)?

> What person or persons in your life matter most to you? With whom would you like to connect at a deeper personal level? What actions will you need to take to accomplish this connection? When will you take them?

> Create your own "don't-do" list. In other words, what actions or attitudes must you take *out* of your life to make room for what matters *in* your life? Set yourself a deadline and make a plan to eliminate some of the habits and behaviors that are holding you back. You may include, on your list, people or things that just are not good for you and need to be removed from your life.

> Now create your "to-do" list. In other words, what are the things you will commit to *start* doing? When will you start?

> What do you most want to learn about? Why do you want to learn about it? How could learning it change your life?

> What do you want to do for certain before your life is over? Why is this important to you?

> If you had to teach some lessons about life to others, what would they be?

> How will you hold yourself accountable to move forward in your life? What kinds of programs or people would be helpful to you in achieving your goals? How can you enroll their support?

STEP THREE. Connect with the important people in your life, and make promises accordingly.

Once you begin to connect with your authentic self and gain clarity about your values, the next step is to share your insights with the important people in your life, the people you trust, who depend on you, who will challenge you, and to whom you are accountable. They may be family members, close friends, or even team members in your workplace with whom you are committed to grow. It makes no difference how large or small this group is. But you must find at least one person with whom you can be honest about your real values. You will inevitably discover that when you risk sharing your innermost desires, these supportive people will help you clarify your values even more. You cannot live your values apart from the world in which you live. You affect others and others affect you.

Take note of other people's values systems as you discover the life you are committed to build together. You can't just explore your values in isolation from the people who depend on you. Discuss your responses to the questions from this exercise with the people in your life.

Finally, decide on the promises you need to make to others. Holding yourself accountable for making specific agreements with others will solidify your connections and increase your self-respect. We suggest you start small. Perhaps pick one or two significant habits that need to be changed in the five most important relationships in your life. Turn these habits into agreements that you can make in the coming year. Then take it one agreement at a time. In relationships, as in life, it is better to have small successes than big failures.

STEP FOUR. Schedule the big rocks first.

In 1967, a man named Charles Hummel wrote a little book called *The Tyranny of the Urgent*. In that book, Hummel makes a vital distinction between "urgent" and "important." On the cusp of the technological age, Hummel saw our society moving into such a demanding time that we would soon become what he called "slaves to the tyranny of the urgent."

Writes Hummel, "The important task rarely must be done today, or even this week. The urgent task calls for instant action. The momentary appeal of these tasks seems irresistible and important, and they devour our energy. But in the light of time's perspective, their deceptive prominence fades. With the sense of loss we recall the vital task we pushed aside. We realize we have become slaves to the tyranny of the urgent."[2]

More than 40 years ago, before cell phones, pagers, text messaging, and emails, he followed this statement with a profound prediction for our time. He foretold that our society, through technology, would make the urgent so accessible that our generation would lose perspective of what is important in a way that no previous generation ever had.

"Urgency" has to do with demands from others that intrude upon you and insist on your immediate attention. "Important" are those things that go beyond the pressing needs of the day and are aligned with the overall direction and focus of your life. When you begin to discern the difference between the "*urgent*" and the "*important*" things in your life, you will find that the important things are, in fact, not "things" at all.

A popular analogy provides further clarification of the distinction between the urgent and the important. Take a moment to stop and visualize three objects: a wide-mouth gallon jar (signifying our lives), a platter of fist-sized rocks (signifying the important aspects of our life), and a bucket of sand (signifying the urgent demands in our lives). If you put the sand in first, there is no room for the rocks, but if you put the rocks in first, the sand will find its way around the rocks.

In short, an accountable life means focusing on your life's "big rocks" at two specific times.

(1)   **Review your "big rocks" on an annual basis.** As we discussed earlier within the section on clarifying your "higher purpose," it is critical to regularly set aside time for a retreat with yourself and the key people in your life for reflection, renewal, and refocusing (we recommend one to two days every year). A great time to do this is just before the New Year, to take an inventory of the previous year and do some planning for the next year and beyond. Ask yourself:

- *How am I doing in relation to living my values?* How would I rate my life (on a scale from one to 10) in each of these areas? What areas need attention in the coming year? What habits need changing? Who can support me

---

[2]Charles E. Hummel, *The Tyranny of the Urgent* (Downers Grove, IL: Intervarsity Press. 1st edition, 1967; rev. ed. 1994.)

in this endeavor? To whom can I be accountable about these issues? These "important" areas are the "big rocks" in your year. To avoid the tyranny of the urgent, be sure to address them first. Answers to the rest of the questions will emerge from this one.

- *How are the important relationships in my life?* Which ones need attention? Where can I create time in my life to nurture these connections? To whom can I be accountable about these relationships?

- *How is my health?* What health habits need changing in the New Year? Where can I find room in my schedule to address these needed changes? Who can help me with this?

- *How much rest and vacation do I need this year?* What would be restful, relaxing, and renewing for me? When, and how much, do I need to schedule time away from work? Who can help me with this?

- *What do I need—and want—to learn this year?* What am I seeking at this time in my life? What courses would I be drawn to take? What books would I like to read? What new relationships—in the form of mentors or teachers— would I like to develop?

- *How is my sense of contribution?* Am I doing enough service—in the world, in my community, and in my family? If the answer is "no," what more can I do, and in what arena?

- *How are my finances?* Do I need to spend less? If I have investments, how are they doing? Am I saving money or spending beyond my means? If I currently have debt, is it manageable? Who can help me with this? What is the truth about my current financial reality? What changes need to be made?

- *What are my problem areas?* If any areas in my life are causing me real problems right now, how can I resolve these issues in the coming year? Am I currently struggling with any addictions; areas in my life that are both destructive and unmanageable? What do I need to do to take care of this? Who can help me?

- *What attention does my business or work need?* (Remember, your business is an opportunity to express yourself, rather than a way to define yourself.) Am I in balance in my work? What areas in my professional life need strengthening or developing? Am I running my work or is my work running me? Who can help me?

Undoubtedly, you will come up with your own practical and meaningful list. Your list is personal to you, your life and your values. Take the time to review it honestly with the key people in your life, and you will avoid the tyranny of the urgent. Take a retreat, at least annually, to look at your life and your work from a higher altitude and from a wider perspective than the day-to-day crises of life.

After this review, you may also want to consider writing a "change list"—a list of what you would like to change about your life this year.

(2) **Review your "big rocks" on a weekly basis.** Set aside 30 minutes before your week begins (Sunday night, for example) to reflect, away from the demands of the world, on what you identified in your annual retreat that needs some attention. Take this time to examine the overall direction of your life in relation to living accountably and authentically. Review how you did in the previous week with regard to living your life in alignment with your values, how you did with your goals, and the challenges you faced. Then take time to record the agreements you have made with yourself and others in each area of importance in your life (e.g., your key relationships, your physical, mental, and spiritual health, and your personal and business development), and schedule time in the coming week to address these agreements with the appropriate actions. This can become the single most important and life-changing habit in your life.

For some areas in your life that need attention, such as a marriage or significant relationship, you may not have to schedule a specific time. Although scheduling weekly dates together could certainly be discussed and recorded, you may simply wish to focus on a certain habit for the week that helps you prioritize, such as a reminder to set the newspaper aside when your spouse needs your attention. However you do this, make the process your own.

Give yourself the flexibility that you need, balanced with firmness in creating what we call "boundaried time" around the areas in your life that need your attention. Examples of "boundaried time" include auto responses on your email, days completely away from the demands of your work, or regular time away from technology so you can focus on people (or refuel in solitude). Remember, if you don't pay attention to what is important in your life, some day these areas will become urgent. Ignore a marriage long enough and one day you will experience the urgency of divorce. Ignore your health and eventually you will experience the urgency of your body's breakdown.

Personal principles only have value when you use them as guideposts for your life's decisions. If you want to know what you value in your life, look at your weekly schedule. You'll see what you really think is important.

STEP FIVE. Take time for daily reflection.

In addition to reviewing your core value areas on an annual and weekly basis, you will want to take time for daily reflection. Choose a time either at the beginning or the end of each day to review the previous day and reflect on the day to come. You should need only five or 10 minutes to consider your plan for the day in terms of your promises to yourself and others, your core values, and your higher purpose.

More and more people are carving out, in their day-to-day lives, time to think, feel, reflect, and listen to the voice within. You should never be so busy that you don't have time to think about what you are doing. Peter Drucker, the management guru, said it best: "There is nothing so useless as doing efficiently that which should not be done at all." To achieve and sustain accountability and alignment of your life with your values, you must step away from your life through these yearly, weekly, and daily reflections. Only with this investment of yourself will your perspective stay focused on the person you are trying to become and the life you are trying to create—beyond the daily tasks and demands from the world.

STEP SIX. Practice integrity in each moment.

Base all decisions on your authentic self, rooted in your center.

Inside each of us there is a sustaining center, a place where all that is most precious to us is embedded. This is our authentic self, what many may refer to as their connection to God or a Higher Power in their life. At our core we find our deepest vulnerability and our greatest strength—what is most sacred to us. This center sustains us, connects us to the comfort we need in times of loss, brings humility in success, adds perspective in chaos, provides strength in weakness, and brings us to wholeness. The structure we offer in this book is a means to a much higher end; it is a *tool* for connecting you to your center.

The real test of accountability lies in each moment. When you are lying in bed early in the morning, debating whether or not to keep that agreement with yourself to get up and exercise, when it's "mind over mattress," what action will you take? When you made an agreement to spend time with your teenage daughter and you get a call from a friend who wants you to play on his baseball team at the same time, what decision will you make? When you have agreed to be more attentive to a spouse, but you'd rather read the newspaper, what will you do? When you have made a commitment to yourself to spend time learning and thinking, but it is easier to get lost in the myriad of emails in your inbox, what do you choose?

STOP—even for a moment—before making any agreement in your life.

The choices you make in those moments require a pause. Before making any new commitment, ask yourself three fundamental questions:

> ➢ Do I have the resources, the capability and the willingness to follow through?
> ➢ Is this agreement in alignment with my internal compass, my authentic self?
> ➢ I know this request may feel urgent, but is it *important*?

If you are not clear about the answers to these questions, give yourself some time. We have all had the experience of saying "yes" to a request, and a moment later kicking ourselves and saying, "What on earth did I do that for?"

The moment-to-moment choices we make determine our true integrity. Integrity will not necessarily bring you the world's approval, but living in line with your conscience always results in self-respect and peace at the end of the day. In those quiet, reflective moments, you face the person in the mirror. This is authentic accountability. We all leave our signature on the world by the decisions we make, one moment at a time. What will yours be?

In the words of Cesar Pavese, the Italian poet, "We do not remember days, we remember moments." Clarity will increase as you continue to practice and strengthen what we call your "integrity muscle." For all of us, it is a lifelong endeavor.

Carry an accountability book with you—everywhere you go.

The final act of integrity, once you make agreements more consciously, is to have a way to keep track of every agreement you make in the course of a day. Whether it's an electronic device or a notebook you carry in your purse or pocket, record every commitment you make immediately. Then, at the end of the day, turn that agreement into a task with a specific deadline attached to it by ensuring that it is entered into your daily planner. Developing this simple habit will help you make agreements more consciously and will give you the freedom of getting them out of your head and placing them on record for follow-up. You don't have to worry about the promises you've made; they will be right there in front of you when the time arrives to honor them.

STEP SEVEN. Create an authentic community to support you and hold you accountable.

Living an authentic, accountable life alone is a difficult endeavor. Connecting with a community means asking yourself some fundamental questions:

> ➤ Who knows me?
> ➤ Who supports me to be more fully who I am meant to be?
> ➤ Who looks beyond my possessions and my roles, my successes and my failures, to who I really am?
> ➤ Who am I accountable to for becoming all I can be?

The price of community is some vulnerability, a risk of rejection, and the intermittent frustration and pain that comes from committing to a relation-

ship for the long haul. The reward of community, however, is the deep fulfillment of belonging to something larger than yourself. You are not alone.

When you are faced with being accountable in unaccountable places,
when you seek to clarify what matters most to you, when your values are
tested under pressure, when you are committed to building an accountable
culture in your organization or family, you'll need a community outside of
that arena from which you can derive support, strength, and perspective. You
need people who care more about your growth than your approval, who will
ask you the hard questions, and hold you to your promises. You need people
whom you trust.

There are many types of relationships that will support your commitment to personal accountability: allies, confidants, mentors, and intimate
relationships, to name a few. Whatever way works for you, and whatever
form a community takes for you, we suggest you be intentional about it;
bear in mind that it's usually easier to create a community than it is to *find*
one. You may have an untapped community right around you, such as a life-
partner to whom you can open up, a colleague, a friend, or an elder in your
life who has walked the path before you.

Start by making a list of your needs from a community. Carefully reflect
upon what you are seeking at this time in your life. Honestly assess the
capability of your current network to be a source of inspiration, support,
and accountability. Be honest with yourself about your commitment to vulnerability. Be intentional about risking deeper connections with the people
already in your life, and on building new bridges with others. A community
can exist as part of an informal but meaningful relationship, or can be a structured group that meets regularly, such as the one David describes below.

Once you step onto the path of accountable, authentic living, it is easy
to get pulled off-course. The pressures to conform, to follow the rewards
of success, to seek security and comfort from external sources, and to drift
back into old familiar habits, can easily result in deviation from core values
and keeping commitments. Having a clear, explicit course of action will be
paramount. By employing the principles discussed so far—seeing blame as a
waste of time, connecting with your authentic self, scheduling the big rocks
first, reflecting daily, practicing integrity in each moment, and building an
authentic community to support you and to hold you accountable—you will
be off to a great start.

DAVID'S STORY: *COMMUNITY IN AGRICULTURE*

For more than two decades I have been involved in supporting authentic communities in agriculture. My clients are ranchers and farmers who are a part of an organization known as Holistic Management, and who consider human beings, their economics, and their environment as inseparable. At the heart of their approach to agriculture lies a simple testing process that enables people to make decisions that simultaneously evaluate financial, social, and environmental realities, both short- and long-term. They consider themselves stewards of the land and of their families, and are changing the landscape of agriculture through more conscious ranching and farming practices.

A significant factor that keeps this organization and its people strong and on-track with its mission are small groups of these grass-roots family businesses that meet regularly in authentic communities to support each other and to hold each other accountable to live their deepest values as a family and in their business. I have known groups that have been meeting monthly for more than 20 years. It is deeply moving and inspiring to see the results of these authentic communities, where people are committed to supporting each other to make decisions that uphold the quality of life they most desire as a family, move through crises, and experience deep personal changes through honesty and accountability.

CHAPTER 4

DEALING WITH UNACCOUNTABLE PEOPLE

Reverend André Scheffer was a minister of the Dutch Reformed Mission Church in Africa. He had a dry sense of humor and liked to poke fun at us. "You know," he would say, "the white man has a more difficult task than the black man in this country. Whenever there is a problem, we (the white man) have to find a solution. But whenever you (blacks) have a problem, you have an excuse. You say 'Ingabilung'... a Xhosa expression that means, 'It is the whites.'"

He was saying that we could always blame all of our troubles on the white man. His message was that we must also look within ourselves and become responsible for our actions—sentiments with which I wholeheartedly agreed.

—NELSON MANDELA

WHERE DO YOU BEGIN IF YOU ARE LIVING or working with someone you perceive to be an unaccountable person? What do you do if you are working in an unaccountable culture? What if you are in a bureaucracy in the middle of the organizational chart? How do you stay accountable? How can you make a difference? How can you start to build an accountable culture—a workplace, a family, or a community—no matter what position you hold? We offer six key strategies, or steps, for staying accountable when you are dealing with a lack of accountability in your workplace, in your community, or in a personal relationship.

JIM'S STORY: *ACCOUNTABILITY IN A FAMILY BUSINESS*

After a day of consulting, a client who had hired us to help his family business with their accountability process, communication, and authentic alignment was driving us to the airport. As he was driving, he started to complain about his brother and his alleged lack of accountability in their partnership.

After listening to the blaming and complaining for a few minutes, I stopped him and asked, "Who is suffering from the actions of your brother?"

"I am, of course," he replied, without any hesitation.

"So, whose problem is it?"

There was a long silence, as I could see him building an internal case that would justify my error in judgment. "I didn't do anything wrong ... *He* made the mistake. How can this be *my* problem?" he asked in disbelief.

"You didn't make the decisions," I acknowledged, "but you are the one suffering the consequences—thus, you are the one who has the problem. And that means that you are the one who must take corrective action. If you expect the person who made decisions to fit *their* needs to solve *your* problem, you will remain stuck."

As he continued to argue with us, building a case for how he was "*right*" and his brother was "wrong," I asked him, "Do you want to be right, or do you want to be *happy?*" With this question, there was a long pause, the pause that comes in the moment of truth, even when you aren't sure you understand what is being said.

"If you want to be happy," I continued, "we suggest you become accountable for your part in the relationship."

THE SIX STEPS FOR STAYING ACCOUNTABLE AROUND UNACCOUNTABLE PEOPLE: *IN BRIEF:*

Step One.   Always start with yourself.

Step Two.   Acquaint yourself with the emergency exits.

Step Three.   Be the change you want to see in the world (Mahatma Gandhi).

Step Four.   Find allies—other accountable people.

Step Five.   Deal directly with unaccountable behavior with clear arguments.

Step Six.   Go for success beyond success.

STEP ONE. Always start with yourself.

In our work of consulting and leading workshops, the most common request we receive is, "How do we get 'those people' to change?" Whether in organizations, communities, or families, virtually all efforts for change into which we are invited have the primary goal of getting other people to be different. The motive is always an ostensibly worthy one, namely "those people" need to change "for the good of themselves and those around them."

The notion of *change* presents an incredible contradiction. Humans, by nature, always seem to want more of something (e.g., love, money, happiness) or less of something (e.g., stress, conflict, worry)—as long as it doesn't mean they themselves have to change.

Even though your reasons for wanting others to change may be noble, the underlying motive is inevitably to control them. Like blaming, focusing your attention on getting others to change is a defense against your own lack of accountability.

Victims—people who expect others to change—are spectators. They live on the sidelines. However, when you look first and foremost at yourself, you put yourself on the playing field. You get into the game. You are no longer watching, criticizing, or complaining. The decision to look at yourself—without blame, but rather with humility—makes you a participant in your life.

It will always be easier to see a lack of accountability in other people. It's always more difficult to see it in yourself. Be honest. If you notice yourself being critical of others, ask yourself what you need to be critical of within *yourself.* Where do *you* fail to keep promises to yourself or others? Where do *you* lack discipline in your life? Where are *you* in need of sharpening your integrity? Where do *you* need to be more courageous? Where do *you* need to be clear about your expectations?

If you have any unaccountable people in your life, we invite you to let these relationships be an opportunity to learn about yourself. Shift the focus (again, not with blame) to yourself. Forget criticism, coercion, or the question, "How do I get them to change?" Instead ask yourself, "What courage is required of *me* right now?" When you make this life-changing shift within yourself, the people around you will change because your perceptions of them will be different. You will find that when you change the way you look at things, the things you look at will change.

One of the great revelations of our time is the awareness that changing your attitudes can change the outer aspects of your life. Changing your perception and beliefs about the world actually changes the world, since changing the world begins with changing yourself. In the words of Stephen Covey, "public victory problems have private victory solutions."

Blaming is contagious, and signifies a lack of accountability in the person doing the blaming. When you are around unreliable people, it's easy to blame them. And guess what? You become part of the problem: you become one of the victims!

DAVID'S STORY: *DEALING WITH A LACK OF ACCOUNTABILITY WITH OWNERSHIP*

I recall very clearly one of the suppliers in our organization with whom we contracted, someone who did not follow through on his promises. When I found myself complaining and blaming this person, Jim brought me right back to accountability:

"Hey, this isn't *his* problem, this is *our* problem. We are the ones who chose to do business with an unaccountable person. We are the ones who made the mistake. And we are the ones who are now accountable to learn from the experience and make new choices."

"If you want to be happy," Jim continued, "we suggest you become accountable for your part in the relationship."

To create accountability around you, you need to bring the focus back to yourself. Don't take the bait: focus on yourself and what you can change, and the behavior of others will lose its power to influence you. Here is a tool that you can use whenever you want to face a problem accountably. Take out a sheet of paper and clearly, at the top of the page, write down the problem. Then draw a line down the middle of the paper. At the top of the left-hand column write: "*Things I can influence or change in this situation, and that need action from me.*" In the right-hand column write: "*Things I have no control over, and that I need to let go of.*" Now get writing. Fill up the page and get to work on the left-hand column, while you let go of the list on the right-hand side. Then track the changes that you see in your life.

STEP TWO. Acquaint yourself with the emergency exits.

The first thing flight attendants do in their orientation on an airplane is point out the location of the emergency exits. You will rarely ever need them, and you certainly don't want to spend much time obsessing about the exits while you're in flight, but it is vital to know where they are when they are required.

In any relationship, whether in your personal or your professional life, you always want to know up front that you can exit if and when you need to. If things get bad enough, if a line is crossed, you always want to know that you can walk away from the situation. Of course, that boundary is going to be different for each person and in each situation, but we all have to have a line. Whether it means you are in danger of compromising your principles, or your safety is in danger, or a particular environment has become toxic to the point of diminishing your health, well-being and authentic self, you need to protect your boundaries. If, for example, you are living in a destructive relationship, or working in an environment that is poisoning you, and you've done all you can to be accountable, and you still cannot find any possibility of a healthy outcome, you will undoubtedly want to think carefully about exiting those situations. Knowing there is an exit creates an assuredness that enables you to work through the rest of the strategies for dealing with unaccountable people, as outlined in the remainder of this chapter. You have the knowledge that if worse comes to worst, you can always cut your losses and leave. Hopefully, you won't get there. But ultimately, *you* are accountable for your life. You can't abdicate that responsibility.

Keep in mind that this is the *emergency* exit—the *final* resort. And remember, don't run for the exit before you learn what you are there to learn and have had the courage to be true to yourself in that relationship. Don't abandon a relationship until you have done everything possible to give that relationship everything you've got. If you use the exit door to escape personal accountability, you will always come up against the same challenge in a later relationship.

We know that leaving a relationship, whether personal or professional, is not easy. Change is difficult, and you may even experience anguish in exiting, whether you are the one leaving or the one being left. So think carefully, learn thoroughly, and act courageously before you head for the exit doors. But always know they are there.

STEP THREE. Be the change you want to see in the world (Mahatma Gandhi).

When you are confronted with unaccountable people in your life, it is unaccountable to start blaming those people, lower your standards to accommodate them, thus sacrificing your values, or exit the relationship prematurely to avoid dealing with them. Fear motivates all these actions, while living accountably requires consciousness and courage.

Whenever you are faced with people on whom you can't rely, stop and take an inventory of your own values and principles. If you want to live accountably, you have to be certain that you are living your values, and that you are not compromising the principles that form the foundation of your own life. Review your own behavior. Be sure that you are living accountably, regardless of whether you are being externally rewarded or even noticed for your choices. Accountability is neither a popularity contest nor a path to social status or approval from others. At the end of the day, living accountably means living in accordance with your conscience, and your degree of personal accountability determines your self-respect, a far greater reward than what the world has to offer.

Accountable people understand that, regardless of their position in an organization or their place in a family, they have an impact on the culture in which they live and work. They understand that they can influence others by the power of their example. So they deliver on their commitments. They keep their standards high, even if they are standards that only they will ever reach. If you want to become accountable, be a giver in the relationship more than a taker. Make a decision to be part of the solution rather than part of the problem. Whatever you do, don't let anyone else turn you into an unaccountable person. If you are relentless about accountability, eventually you will find yourself surrounded by people who respect and support your values. Along the way, you will live with self-worth and the world around you will change because you are changing.

STEP FOUR. Find allies—other accountable people.

> *Oh, the comfort, the inexpressible comfort of feeling safe with a person, having neither to weigh thoughts nor measure words, but pouring them all out, just as they are, chaff and grain together, certain that a faithful hand will take and sift them, keep what is worth keeping, and with the breath of kindness blow the rest away.*
> —George Eliot

Living accountably, in accordance with your deepest principles and core values independent of the culture that surrounds you, is a lonely journey, and it cannot be done alone. We need allies—support in the truest sense—along the way. Aligning with and connecting to allies is not necessarily about finding a person who agrees with your point of view. A true ally is a person you open up to, confide in, and trust. Finding and choosing an ally means asking, "Who supports me?" "To whom am I accountable?" "Who will support me to keep my promises?"

An ally can be either inside or outside your organization. You may have an ally that is supporting you to build accountability in a significant personal relationship. The goal is to support you and hold you accountable for living honorably in your current reality. Rather than giving answers, allies help guide you to your own truth. They affirm you and care about you without necessarily agreeing with you. They are not afraid to be honest and are able to do so without diminishing you. They help expose you to the truth that lies behind your blind spots; they offer hope, but they don't tell you how or whether to proceed. They hold you accountable to live out what matters most in your life. They seek to provide perspective and help you find and change your old familiar patterns without seeking approval or comfort. Allies will occasionally pull you up by the collar to a place that is high enough for you to see your life from a new viewpoint. The Sufis had it right when they said, "The eye can't see itself." We need others to help us find new ground to stand on and new eyes to see the view.

One of the most beautiful qualities of true friendship is to understand and to be understood. True allies are very precious. To think you can take the authentic and accountable journey without allies is like thinking you can survive a Canadian winter without a coat.

STEP FIVE. Deal directly with unaccountable behavior with clear agreements.

When confronted with a perceived lack of accountability around you, you are left with, essentially, three choices: (a) Ignore it, which will eventually turn into a toxic environment: disrespect, resentment, and frustration that goes underground and surfaces indirectly in the form of gossip, criticism, and complaining; (b) Take personal accountability in the form of strategies that we have discussed this far in this section. The result of personal accountability is always increased self-respect, confidence, and compassion, even in the midst of a sick environment; or (c) Deal directly with the unaccountable behavior with the use of clear agreements.

The strategy of dealing directly with unaccountable people implies that you first take personal accountability. You can then take it one step further with the unaccountable person by saying, in essence, "We have an apparent misunderstanding and I'd like to take ownership for my part of the problem by clarifying my agreements to you and my expectations from you." If this kind of approach seems the appropriate response, then Chapter 7 will give you a practical and simple process for going to the next step of writing these agreements down for even further clarification. Clarity about expectations often transforms conflict into a solution. Frequently what is judged as unaccountable behavior is simply a matter of misunderstanding what is expected, what is needed for support, and the consequences of both honoring and disregarding promises made.

STEP SIX. Go for success beyond success.

Reading thus far, you may have gotten the impression that if you become an accountable person everything will work out just the way you want it to. If you are thinking that personal accountability will result in you getting a great boss, big contracts, promotions, a blissful marriage (and parking spaces wherever you want), let us assure you this is not the case. Although accountable living may increase your probability for some of these things, it doesn't guarantee you any of these results. If you are seeking success only in material terms, you will be disappointed in accountability. If you expect the world to operate on your terms, you are in for many disappointments.

We like what Fred Kofman says about this:

> *"You are accountable for your life" can be a baited hook. It is true enough to sound appealing and untrue enough to cause great confusion. It is empowering to see yourself as a contributor to the problem—and thus a contributor to the solution. Yet it is dangerous to see yourself as the sole creator of results that also depend on external circumstances.*
>
> *Paradoxically, assuming accountability for results can create as much pain as avoiding accountability for your behavior. When you choose to step up to the plate, you naturally feel that things should work out. However, even the best hitters strike out most of the time … To face life's challenges accountably, you navigate between two hazards. At one extreme lies the self-soothing explanation of the victim—'I have nothing to do with my situation.' At the other lies the unrealistic omnipotence of the superhero—'I am the sole creator of my reality.'"*[1]

So just how do you navigate these hazards? You do so by making a decision to live your life in accordance with your deepest principles and core values, and in the process, you experience what Kofman calls "success beyond success." When you act with integrity, when you bring accountability to your life, regardless of your circumstances, when you know within yourself that you are an accountable person, even if no one around you appreciates or even acknowledges it, you connect with and express your higher, authentic self. You might not always achieve success as it is measured by external results, but you can always behave *honorably*—which is what we call *internal* success, a success that is enduring.

The reward of accountable living, then, is not success by society's standards, but rather the freedom, self-respect, and peace of mind that come from living authentically. This kind of inner success gives you the structural integrity needed to hold up the challenges you face in life with passion and confidence as you build bridges over the white water rapids you encounter.

---

[1]Fred Kofman, *Conscious Business: How to Build Value Through Values*, Boulder, CO: Sounds True Publication, 2006, 64–65.

Victor Frankl, a Jewish psychiatrist and Holocaust survivor, spoke of this freedom when he wrote, "We who lived in concentration camps can remember the men who walked through the huts comforting others, giving away their last piece of bread. They may have been few in number, but they offer sufficient proof that everything can be taken from a person but one thing: the last of the human freedoms—the freedom to choose one's attitude in any given set of circumstances—to choose one's own way ... It is this spiritual freedom—which cannot be taken away—that makes life meaningful and purposeful."[2]

Adherence to a code of internal ethics gives you credibility with yourself, which leads to greater self-respect and eventual confidence in the marketplace and beyond. *You* are the starting place for building an accountable culture or relationship. Life hands you many situations beyond your control; living accountably gives you the power to choose how you respond. Accountable living is a passport to freedom, giving you the power and the courage to change the things you can, while accepting the things that are beyond your control. The Christophers, a Christian organization, have chosen powerful words of personal accountability as their motto: "It is better to light one candle than to curse the darkness."

We conclude this chapter on dealing effectively with unaccountable people with a quote inscribed at the tomb of an Anglican Bishop in Westminster Abbey. We feel that this statement epitomizes our philosophy of personal accountability:

> *"When I was young and free and my imagination had no limits, I dreamed of changing the world; as I grew older and wiser I discovered the world would not change, so I shortened my sights somewhat and decided to change my country, but it too seemed immovable. As I grew into my twilight years, in one last desperate attempt, I settled for changing only my family, those closest to me. But alas, they would have none of it!*
>
> *And now I realize as I lie on my death bed, if I had only changed myself first, then, by example, I might have changed my family. From their aspirations and encouragement I would have then been able to better my country, and who knows, I might have even changed the world."*

---

[2]Victor E. Frankl, *Man's Search for Meaning*, New York, NY: Washington Square Press, Simon and Schuster, 1963. 1st ed., 1946; rev. ed., 2006.

CHAPTER 5

FINDING COMMON GROUND ACROSS GENERATIONS THROUGH ACCOUNTABILITY

DURING ONE OF OUR SESSIONS with a group of leaders in a financial services firm, several partners lamented, "The problem with our workplace today is that young people joining our firm want to be a partner within five years, and only want to work 35 hours a week!" Other partners reacted on behalf of those young people—their direct reports—by saying, "Yes, but they may feel we have worked way too hard, have centered our lives in our work, have no quality of life, and are stuck in outdated ways of doing business." So who's right, and how are we to find common ground?

Today, more than ever, we have a diverse age range in the workplace, where four or more generations now work side-by-side. Each generation brings their own set of prejudices, opinions, values, and beliefs to the workplace. Often, each generation possesses distinct attitudes derived from the social, political, and economic climate of their youth—and the meaning made of their experiences along the way. If you are managing people with differing values, those differences may result in conflict. Accountability, as a shared core value, can bridge that generation gap. By focusing on the similarities between the generations, and on the value that each generation can bring to the world of work, differences can be reconciled.[1]

In many instances, the younger generation will not comfortably tolerate what they perceive to be an outdated, command-and-control type of traditional management practice. This intolerance can be beneficial, because it may offer the Baby Boomers a new perspective, one which will teach them to take better care of themselves and to be more responsible for their own well-being. Conversely, the "nose to the grindstone" attitude often embraced by older generations can model the value of a positive work ethic and the rewards it brings with respect to self-esteem, teamwork, and financial benefits.

In other words, the generations can help each other find balance. But first they have to open their minds to the other's way of seeing things. Discussion about accountability can facilitate that process. Anyone would agree, for example, that punctuality and quality work on projects are positive attributes, regardless of whether the person agreeing is a senior vice-president in his fifties, or a 20-something clerk. Punctuality and quality work signify a commitment to *accountability* in the workplace, and everyone wants that. Accountability is where discussion about the work itself and about everyone's expectations of each other can begin, and resolution on other issues can emerge as a result of such discussion.

David's Story: "No Good Time" is an example of a clash in perspectives. In this example, the sales manager could have offered the VP a plan for accountability to which the younger manager had committed before going on holiday. The plan would spell out the younger manager's accountabilities, and a timeframe for when each of those accountabilities would be completed, *taking his holidays into consideration.* Such an agreement would

---

[1]We are aware that the differences we are discussing are not always generational. Clearly, people of the same generation can have very different philosophies as a result of their different life experiences. We think we can generalize somewhat, however, that the work ethic of the Baby Boomer generation was somewhat less focused on family and home-life balance, and more focused on "getting ahead" at work and building financial security through longer work hours resulting in less time with the family. The younger generation, in our experience, seems to be rebelling against that "nose to the grindstone" work ethic and trying to find more time for family and life outside of work. We know that these generalizations have substantial numbers of people as exceptions. For the sake of discussion, in this chapter we are drawing a philosophical line between the generations, in hopes that we can offer solutions for bridging the gap.

DAVID'S STORY: *"NO GOOD TIME"*

In the midst of a recent conversation with a sales manager, who is in his forties, his vice-president of sales, who is in his late-fifties, interrupted us. Obviously irritated, he asked the whereabouts of one of his young managers, who is in his early twenties.

"Where's Jason?" the VP inquired, clearly annoyed.

"He's on vacation," the sales manager replied. "Don't you remember? He let you know last month that he would be away this week with his wife and young daughter."

"What's he doing going on holiday now? Doesn't he know it's a terrible time?"

The sales manager's response was interesting.

"Yes, Bob, it is a terrible time. And it would have been a terrible time last week, and the week before that, and the week before that ..."

---

demonstrate to the older manager that the younger manager had not compromised the needs of the workplace in favor of his personal life, but rather had taken responsibility for those workplace needs by finding a way to meet them in conjunction with taking his holidays. (Such written accountability agreements are the topic of Chapter 7.) Communication about that accountability agreement with the older manager would have assuaged his concerns that the younger manager's work ethic and attitude were poor. It would also have modeled to him the possibility of a *work-home-life balance*, a potentially threatening but also beneficial idea for him to consider for himself.

The different generations can achieve a work-lifestyle balance if they are committed to come together in the spirit of openness, good-will, and inquiry. We believe a new definition of loyalty can emerge, based on direct and respectful communication, commitment to and follow-through on promises, clear and considered priorities, and trust.

In-depth conversations about expectations, needs, contribution, loyalty, and meaning can bridge the gap between different philosophies in the workplace. It requires dialogue and understanding rather than criticism, for each generation has much to learn from and much to offer the other. Accountable people, regardless of their age, can take the lead in building the bridge.

Surviving and thriving into the next generation—while creating cultures that attract and retain great people across generations—will depend on transcending knee-jerk reactions and first impressions to reach a deeper common understanding and workable system within the organization. Finding unity through commitment to accountability can leverage these differences to transform conflict into the birth of new possibilities, and ultimately, into the development of extraordinary organizations.

LESSONS FROM FAMILIES IN BUSINESS

JIM'S STORY: *A NEW KIND OF CEO*

I recently facilitated a family meeting with three generations and 35 family members ranging in age from 16 to ninety-one. Here is what occurred:

I was preparing for my presentation at a resort, and as I surveyed the room, the differences in the generations became obvious. At one end of the room were a couple of young people listening to iPods and talking on cell phones while simultaneously carrying on conversations with the other young people nearby. In another corner of the room were the 40-somethings—talking on their Blackberries, text messaging, and conversing about various problems and opportunities in the business. Another group, in their fifties and sixties, were sitting around discussing golf and their kids. The final group members, in their seventies and older, were sitting alone wondering why they were invited to the meeting in the first place.

The focus of this meeting was to create a shared vision for the family and the business that would hopefully become a beacon for generations to come. We started the meeting with a lively discussion about values. I soon noticed that as each person spoke they looked across the room at Grandma, almost as though they were seeking her approval or her endorsement for their point of view. In most cases she never said anything. Instead, at most of the comments, she simply smiled.

At the break I asked a couple of the younger people why everyone was always looking at Grandma. They quickly responded, "Oh, Grandma is the CEO of our family. I thought you knew that."

"The CEO, Grandma?" I inquired.

"Yes, she is the Chief Emotional Officer in the family. Everyone from Grandpa on down understands that she is the glue that keeps this family together."

At that moment, I realized that families who are successful in transitioning their business over many years and across many generations offer lessons as to how leadership in a culture can, in fact, transcend vast age differences. Grandma is seldom technically savvy or politically correct, but all the generations go to her and respect her. Why? Because she personifies the qualities of a true authentic leader. She loves and cares for each member of the family; she appreciates their individuality, their special unique gifts. She is aware of each person's passions and she supports them in pursuing them. She trusts them to make decisions that are right for them, but that are also in the best interests of the family as a whole. Grandma works for the betterment of the whole family. She listens carefully to each family member, and only expresses her opinion when asked (which I observed over the months of working with this family to be a frequent occurrence!). Yet, when asked for her opinion, she responds primarily with, "Well, what do you think you should do?" or "What do you think about that?"

She is authentic leadership in its finest form, ultimately inspiring other members of the family to be authentic themselves.

We have discovered that the challenge of integrating multiple generations is not unique to large organizations. We have a large number of clients who have been merging generations successfully for many years and can thus provide perspective and guidance in this area. Who are these organizations that have succeeded in building sustainable workplaces by tapping into the resources and wisdom of each generation? Successful family businesses— the eight to 10 per cent who make it beyond the second generation—have found a way to nurture and foster accountability across many generations, and with this challenge comes enormous opportunity. In successful family business we have often witnessed strength in mentoring, personal growth, loyalty and dedication to a single employer, shared visioning, teamwork, meaningful contribution, and the building of a legacy—all of which require accountability from each person. These strengths are the results of companies recognizing, supporting, and capitalizing on the wisdom and strength of each generation. These companies have adapted behavioral strategies to minimize potential conflicts, and offer us wisdom for building accountability across generations.

There are lessons here for dealing with multiple generations. Here's what we have observed these successful family businesses doing, and what they can teach leaders in today's workplace who are dealing with multi-generations:

ONE. Successful family businesses have a deep respect for, and commitment to, people.

Two fundamental beliefs form the foundation of successful family businesses. *First*, they believe that every person, regardless of their age and perspective, has something to offer and therefore they focus on people's strengths, not weaknesses. They are committed to *fit* people rather than *fix* people. *Second*, they believe that accountability and the resulting understanding of commitment are built through contribution rather than entitlement. They don't just offer their younger employees a free ride; they require them to contribute, and thereby engender accountability in them. By doing so, they foster an environment where young people participate and feel themselves part of the system. Accountability comes from *being needed*, rather than from *needing*. Young people who have been raised to give rather than take have the necessary strength of character to foster growth into the next generation.

Authentic leadership is about identifying those values that cross all generational lines and then having the leaders actually live those values, just like Grandma did. Our question for you is, "Who is Grandma—the Chief Emotional Officer—in your organization? Who is accountable for connection? Who is accountable for ensuring that those values and principles that transcend generational diversity are recognized and practiced?"

TWO. Successful family businesses practice consistent and sincere listening.

Successful family businesses put the values of caring and respect into action by consistently listening to each other's feelings, aspirations, values, perspectives, and desires—through meetings and informal conversations. They continuously negotiate so that both the needs of the organization and the wishes of the family members are met, both in and out of the business.

Respect offered to the younger generation—by valuing them as genuine contributors—is reciprocated to the elders through listening to their wisdom and experience. Mentoring is integral to the development of accountability and to the subsequent succession of the business. There are few experiences more rewarding than to see two or more generations working together, side-by-side, parents passing on to their successors their craft, and successors listening carefully and learning from their failures because they are encouraged rather than criticized.

Consistent and sincere listening can engender trust, new wisdom, and synergy. For example, by setting aside preconceived ideas and assumptions about self-centeredness and laziness on the part of younger people, members of the older generation may discover—through nonjudgmental listening— that those younger people are just trying to find balance between their work and their personal lives. Conversely, younger people may learn through listening that the Baby Boomer work ethic is not entirely dogmatic, but rather an attempt to create value in their lives through hard work and solid effort. Through listening, both generations may discover that they are seeking the same result—working smart and having time for joy and family and other good things in life—despite differing approaches.

THREE. Successful family businesses are authentic.

In successful business families, people are respected for who they are. There is congruence between who they are personally and who they are professionally. They don't have to check who they are at the door when they come to work. They are supported, in every generation, to contribute to the family and to the business through the expression of their unique, authentic self. Successful business families teach us that you have an accountability to produce results but you also have an accountability to make an emotional connection both in the family and in the business. They care about each person, and don't attempt to manipulate others into being people they are not.

They respect each other's differences, encourage those around them to follow their dreams, and support them in their pursuit of authenticity. And if that means leaving the business, then the foundation has been built to allow them to do so. Of course, as in any business, no family is perfect, people are not always comfortable with each other, and conflict often arises. But the overall system rests on a foundation of respect, commitment, and an emphasis on the people.

Jim describes the culture at Hewlett Packard, where he spent years in a senior management capacity, as that of a "family," where you felt that you belonged to something much bigger than a place where you simply picked up a paycheck. The parallel between families in business and developing accountability in a multi-generational organization can only go so far, but we hope it is useful to you as we turn our attention in the next chapter to how personal accountability can take root and grow within the family.

CHAPTER 6

DEVELOPING ACCOUNTABLE YOUNG PEOPLE
HOW TO LAUNCH YOUR KIDS SUCCESSFULLY

JUST AS AN ACCOUNTABLE CULTURE begins with personal accountability, the foundation of personal accountability is established in one's upbringing. We are not born accountable; we have to develop this trait. Though it is not impossible to acquire as an adult, it is difficult. This chapter outlines some practical principles and practices for developing accountable young people. You don't have to be a parent to find value in this section of the book. If you are an uncle, aunt, coach, teacher, supervisor, good friend or neighbor to young people, we hope you will find our perspective valuable. While we will be primarily talking about parenting in this chapter, substitute any role you may have with young people for the word parent in the forthcoming pages. If you are committed to influencing our future generation, then you are embarking on what we feel is the most important leadership work on the planet: developing capable, accountable youth.

Let us say right up front that we are not experts in raising kids. We are especially not experts in raising *your* kids. Although David has been a family therapist, scout leader, parent, and grandparent, and has a university degree in child development, and Jim has worked with kids and has been a parent for more than 35 years, we have both learned and continue to learn from the children in our lives. We trust that our observations, insights, and practical ideas about accountability will be useful as you reflect on the vital accountability you have to the young people in your life. We also know that hindsight brings clarity and that no one parents perfectly. Parenting is a lifetime apprenticeship from which you never graduate. Please see our perspective as a vision for parenting (maybe even grandparenting) to inspire you and move you to action.

There is certainly no need to act on all of our ideas. From the smorgasbord of insights we offer, choose one or two key ideas that seem the most relevant at this stage of your parenting vocation, and start there.

We begin with three fundamental accountabilities of a parent in order to foster accountability within your children.

FUNDAMENTAL ACCOUNTABILITIES OF A PARENT: *IN BRIEF*

> **Accountability One.** You are accountable for the environment in your home, not for your children's happiness.
>
> **Accountability Two.** You are accountable for establishing a climate in your home that balances *supports* and *demands*.
>
> **Accountability Three.** You are accountable for building strong relationships with your children, assisting them in finding positive adult role models to connect with, while inspiring and guiding them to find their own authentic voice.

FUNDAMENTAL ACCOUNTABILITIES OF A PARENT: *DISCUSSION*

ACCOUNTABILITY ONE. You are accountable for the environment in your home, not for your children's happiness.

Ask yourself the following questions, "What are my beliefs about raising children?" "What do I really want for our children?" "What values and virtues do we want them to leave home with?"

If you are co-parenting, it is well-advised to discuss your answers with your partner. Take some time to reflect on these questions. Talk about them as a family. Share your goals regarding parenting with your kids (at an age-appropriate level). It will help you articulate your own vision and purpose as a parent.

Over the past few years, David has made it a point to ask parents in his sessions, "How many of you would identify *happiness* as one of your top three desires for your kids?" With this generation's desire to be more sensitive and responsive to the needs of children, the vast majority of parents in each audience consistently raise their hands.

This might well be one of the main differences between this generation of parents and previous generations, and may well be contributing to the extended time that young people now remain in our homes. Parents of previous generations probably didn't worry so much about their children's happiness. They probably didn't sit in the kitchen after they sent you to your room, agonizing over whether they had destroyed your self-esteem. If you are over 45 and your parents are still alive, ask them what their goals were for you when you were being raised. There is a good chance that making you "happy" was not on their list of goals.

When I asked this of my mother in her seventy-seventh year, her reply was, "Happiness? We never thought about it much. We believed if you learned and lived good values, then happiness would result. Whether you were happy or not was not the issue. It wasn't our job to make you happy. Besides, happiness is not a destination. Happiness is a method of travel." Most of the Baby Boomers—those of us over the age of 45—would not dare tell our parents we were bored or unhappy because we knew if we did, in all likelihood they would put us to work.

Regardless of what you decide the most important goals are for your children, we suggest you take happiness off your list. When your children are unhappy, bored, or angry, remember it's not your job as a parent to turn this around. Instead, encourage them to accept life on life's terms and to take responsibility to find their own happiness along the way. Removing happiness from your list of goals for your kids not only makes your job easier and less stressful as a parent, it also shifts the accountability for being happy back to your children. As Abraham Lincoln said, "I'm as happy as I make up my mind to be." If you yourself are an accountable person, you might not be happy all the time, but you will be a generally happy person. Be a model for happiness yourself, and let your children take their cue from you.

ACCOUNTABILITY TWO. You are accountable for establishing a climate in your home that balances *supports* and *demands*.

You, as a parent, have an accountability to create an environment where children feel supported. Without support, you invite resentment and decreased confidence, not accountability. Along with support, you also have an accountability to ensure that your kids are not overly sheltered from the demands of life. To be mature adults, they need to learn how to deal with what life hands them.

Parents of young people today may well be the first generation committed to both of these tasks. Prior to the 1940s, life in the home was primarily about survival. There was no time and little awareness of the importance of a child's self-esteem, confidence, or happiness.

World War II and the horrors of the Holocaust ushered in a new era and a new consciousness to the western world. The Fifties and Sixties were a time of growing affluence and the emergence of the psychological age where self-esteem, personal growth, and the "Me Generation" arose from the repressive era of survival and hard work. Many parents who raised children in this new psychological era, and who came from these homes with too much demand and not enough support, found themselves saying when they had children, "I'm not going to raise my children the way I was raised. I want to protect my children from the pain and demands I had as a child. I am going to ensure that my child has self-esteem, confidence, and happiness."

The intent to safeguard our children from the wounds of our own past is a worthy one, and one that moves us forward, but if you combine this intent with smaller families, increased affluence, and the goal of happiness, you end up with a generation of spoiled young people, raised with too much support and not enough demands. Adolescence extending into one's thirties and failure to launch our children into adulthood is a result of families out of balance.

Even though outwardly it may appear that children raised during the Depression had more accountability, the task of parents today is not to go back to the "good old days" of survival, the old work ethic, and a lack of consideration for the emotional needs of our children. Nor is it our task to rescue our children from the pains of life. The task today is to chart new territory by making a commitment to raise our children with both support *and* demands. Every day we must ask ourselves as parents, "Does this child in front of me need support or does this child need to be pushed? How can I be there for him or her, offering support to deal with whatever demands arise—with love but without a need to rescue?"

Take a moment to stop and assess where you are on the Support/ Demand continuum. Every parent seems better at one than the other, and every parent can expand his or her capacity to learn about the other side of the equation. In our guiding principles for raising healthy and accountable children outlined later, we hope you will find a healthy balance between *supports* and *demands*.

DAVID'S STORY: *HIS MOTHER'S REAL HARDSHIPS*

My mother grew up in a 900-square-foot farmhouse along with seven other siblings. There were days when all they had to eat was potatos. She started school in 1927 and had to ride six miles on horseback to get there. In grade one, Joyce got strapped by a teacher. "Do you think I would have even dared to complain to my father? And with him working three jobs, do you think he would have even thought of getting back on that horse to ride six miles to the school for a parent-teacher conference? No way. No one in my family ever found out about that strapping until years later. At that time, I learned that this was *my* problem, not the teacher's or my parents'. It was my responsibility."

This example illustrates a fairly typical family of that age that was out of balance by today's standards. Joyce got strapped in school, received no support, and was left feeling that the responsibility was hers, rather than her caregivers'. This example demonstrates an environment that was out of balance and filled with an excess of demand with little support.

ACCOUNTABILITY THREE. You are accountable for building strong relationships with your children, assisting them in finding positive adult role models to connect with, while inspiring and guiding them to find their own authentic voice.

When David was practicing as a family therapist, a corporate lawyer brought in his 15-year-old son for therapy. The boy had been charged with shoplifting, breaking-and-entering, and damaging public property. After struggling for an hour trying to get this bright kid to open up and talk about what was behind these self-destructive actions, the father finally looked across the room and, with tears in his eyes, asked, "Do you think it is too late to start spending time with my son?"

Children find mirrors through which they define themselves in the eyes and attitudes of the parents, teachers, and other adults in their lives. If these mirrors are absent in the home, they will look for a reflection wherever they can find it. Who is reflecting back *your* children's worth? How much of a priority are your children in your life? Even though you may have children that are born with a temperament that is tough to bond with, as a parent you are accountable for your part in this relationship, and to find healthy adult role models they can connect with.

Children have enormous wisdom within them. There are times when they need direction and answers from adults, but most importantly, they need adults to take time to listen and help them access their own inner awareness. This is a skill that requires a lifetime of practice, beginning when children are born. As we intentionally support young people to think for themselves, to problem-solve using their inner resources, and to trust their own wisdom, we are preparing them to live authentic, capable, and accountable adult lives long after we, as caregivers, are out of the picture.

We've all heard that you can lead a horse to water, but you can't make it drink. While there is truth in this principle, what you *can* do is put salt in the oats by investing in those relationships.

Below is a list of practical reminders for developing the kind of relationships with children that foster accountability. If you keep these guiding principles in mind as you go through day-to-day living, you are likely to find your relationships with your children improving over time.

NINE GUIDING PRINCIPLES FOR RAISING HEALTHY AND ACCOUNTABLE CHILDREN: *IN BRIEF*

Principle One.   Make time to simply *be* with your children—when you have no expectations or agenda.

Principle Two.   Give your children wings—by helping them find their *own* strength.
a. Build self-worth through dialogue.
b. Encourage your children without rescuing them.
c. Build self-trust through self-affirmation.

Principle Three.   Implement scheduled processes to create a strong and accountable family.
a. Create meaningful rituals in your family.
b. Hold weekly accountability sessions to organize household chores.
c. Go beyond chores to *contribution*.

Principle Four.   Balance "rights" with "accountabilities."

Principle Five.   Teach your children about limits.

Principle Six.   Don't be blinded by your children's pain.

Principle Seven.   Be a light, not a judge.

Principle Eight.   Maintain perspective.

Principle Nine.   Let go.

NINE GUIDING PRINCIPLES FOR RAISING HEALTHY AND ACCOUNTABLE CHILDREN: *DISCUSSION*

PRINCIPLE ONE. Make time to simply *be* with your children—when you have no expectations or agenda.

Many people come to our parenting talks wanting quick fixes about how they can get their kids to do their homework, clean their rooms, keep their promises, and take more initiative in their lives. Our response is that the foundation of "getting" your child to do anything is built on a relationship of "giving," where you spend time *not* trying to get them to do something.

If you are seeing unaccountable behavior in your children, ask yourself how much time you take with each child in your family, individually, when there are no expectations, only mutually enjoyable activities. The core of accountability is feeling loved and noticed in the world—not for what we do but for who we are. A wise grandmother said it best when she told us that love in the family is spelled *t-i-m-e*.

PRINCIPLE TWO. Give your children wings—by helping them find their *own* strength.

a. Build self-worth through dialogue.

In 1930, 70 per cent of all North Americans lived on farms or in small rural communities. Today, more than 90 per cent of our population lives in cities. This drastic change over two generations has brought with it radical change in how people relate to each other. Families have moved from living rooms filled with conversation to family rooms loaded with electronic devices. Dialogue has diminished from conversation around the supper table, kitchen clean-up, and farm chores, to rooms filled with screens that discharge noise and images that discourage interpersonal connection.

Developing accountability in young people requires dialogue: engaging, meaningful interaction in a supportive and safe environment of sincere mutual interest. In families detached from each other, you find people constantly doing their own thing, each with their own computers, televisions, iPods, and handheld video games, with little time for any real conversation. Even though there is a place for such devices in the lives of young people, we need to balance high-tech with high touch. In disengaged families that are out of balance, contact is often initiated by crisis, and takes the form of directing, lecturing, threatening, correcting, explaining, or rescuing.

Take the time to listen carefully without judgment. Ask open-ended questions, explore options, and guide your children to discover their own truth. Learn to feel with your children, to open your heart, to express your love and concern directly, and to tune in to their emotions or needs without rescuing or anesthetizing them with quick fixes. To achieve dialogue, take the time to open up, share yourself, check in, and be present.

In addition, to support your children, start at an early age to help them find their own inner wisdom—while guiding them to make healthy decisions. You can respect their view of the world and the choices they make without always agreeing with them. Of course there will be times when you must step in, set limits and say "no." As their parent, you can see their lives with more perspective, and you certainly need to overrule morally wrong or self-destructive decisions. But when you listen and respect them enough to support their feelings and their needs, affirm them as human beings with a right to their opinion, and explore with them the pros and cons of their options while guiding them to make their own decisions, you cultivate a relationship in which accountability can grow.

Here are a few suggestions for getting your kids to open up with you:

> *Start young.* Making room for open, trusting dialogue takes practice and time. Like any investment, the earlier you start, the greater your return long-term.

> *Start with yourself.* No matter what the age, openness begets openness. Don't push your children to open up. Invite them by talking about yourself, even about simple things that happen to you during the day and your emotional response to those experiences.

> *Set aside a regular time for connecting.* Until adolescence, a child needs a daily time for connection. A quiet time that invites sharing right after school, around the supper table, or at bedtime are often opportune moments. Adolescents, no matter what they tell you, need a time at *least* once a week, if not daily, of undivided attention from a significant adult who values them enough to listen to what's going on in their lives and explore ways of finding their own truth. Even when you don't get an answer to a question, don't let this be a deterrent from continuing to ask.

> *Respect each child's age and uniqueness.* Preschoolers, until they are verbal, often open up more readily through art. You can often get young children to express their emotions by having them draw a picture of the feelings they may be experiencing. Adolescents also often open up through writing. Your children will *teach* you their way of opening up if you tune in. Watching how they open up with their friends is a clue for how they might open up with you.

> *Ask open-ended questions—and don't react judgmentally.* When children begin to express a feeling, instead of jumping in with a quick reaction, it is often helpful to explore a deeper understanding. After any experience, either a success or a failure, the following kind of exploring questions can be useful: "What is

your understanding of what happened? What might have caused that to happen? What did you learn from the experience? What action(s) can you take next time, based on this new learning?"

➢ *Encourage personal writing.* When your son or daughter reaches early adolescence, buy them a journal, and don't ever violate their trust by reading it without their permission. Validate their feelings by supporting them to write without feeling the pressure to share everything with you. If a child knows you respect his privacy, he is more likely to write—and, ultimately, to trust you.

➢ *Respect your child's need for space.* Some kids need more time alone than others. Be sensitive when they withdraw, and ask to be invited in to their space. Honest expression can only happen in an environment of respect and acceptance.

DAVID'S STORY: *TAKING THE TEMPERATURE THROUGH A FAMILY COUNCIL*

In my upbringing our family had a habit of weekly family council sessions and when my children were born, I continued this tradition. Every Sunday morning, we take about 30 minutes to meet for a weekly "pow-wow." We have been doing this for years, since our children were in preschool. The agenda is as follows:

1. **A Silent Moment or Prayer to start.**
2. **Weekly temperature reading:** How are people feeling this week? What bouquets—appreciations—do you have for anyone or anything in the family? Who needs recognition this week? Whose needs are not being met? Does anyone have a problem or concern to discuss? What were our successes in the past week (individually and/or collectively)? What support does anyone need? What are we grateful for? What goals are people working on? How about dreams? What complaints do people have? (Note: All complaints are to be accompanied by a recommendation.)
3. **Accountability Session:** (This is a check-in for how chores and promises are coming along.) Once a month we have a "chore session" where we list the upcoming chores and assign responsibilities to each one, from paying the mortgage to cleaning toilets. Then, in the Accountability Session, we do a check-in to see how everyone is doing in relation to the fulfillment of our agreements. What requests need to be made? What adjustments

are necessary? How are we all doing with our respective Accountability Agreements? (We have found if you let *agreements* govern the family, rather than rules, it builds accountability and respect, and takes some of the pressure off the parents to always have to be the "chore police." Our goal, as parents, is to be *facilitators* and *guides* with our children, rather than *dictators* and *tyrants*.)

4. **Family virtue of the week.** Using Linda Popov's book, *The Family Virtue Guide*,[1] we read, study and discuss one virtue that we focus on for the coming week. The simple strategies outlined in this book are applicable to children of any age and have been a source of inspiration to us for many years.

5. **Parent Report Card.** As a father, I have negotiated with my daughters, a list of virtues that I am accountable for living in our home. They include:

   - **Respectful**—Do my children feel loved, trusted, and respected by me?
   - **Kind**—Do they feel I am thoughtful, caring, and considerate?
   - **Accountable**—Can I be counted on when I make a promise?
   - **Honesty**—Do I tell the truth, in the family and outside the home?
   - **Fun**—Do we laugh together?
   - **Relaxed**—Is it comfortable, calm, and peaceful to be around me?
   - **Available**—Am I available and accessible when I am needed? Do my children feel I can relate to them and what they are going through?

   Every few months my daughters give me a report card on each of these areas, including the grades, comments, and recommendations. This experience, over the years, has truly been an enriching, engaging, learning, and fun opportunity for all of us, not only in coming up with the criteria in which to measure their father, but also in the rich dialogue that follows.

6. **A Silent Moment or Prayer, along with an expression of gratitude to end.**

As the children grow and find interests outside the home, it becomes increasingly difficult to consistently adhere to our habit of weekly family council sessions. We still keep at it though and get it in when we can. And even if people complain when it is time to call the meeting to order, we all know it is good for our family.

---

[1] Linda K. Popov, *The Family Virtues Guide: Simple Ways To Bring Out The Best In Our Children and Ourselves*, New York, NY: A Plume Book, 1997.

b. Encourage your children without rescuing them.

"You can do it, and I'm here to support you." "I believe in you." "I know you can handle this." These are all fundamental messages that young people need if they are going to be accountable. Jonas Salk, the great scientist who discovered the polio vaccine, understood the concept of being encouraging.

He was once asked, "How does this outstanding achievement, which has effectively brought an end to the word 'polio' in our vocabulary, cause you to view your previous 200 failures?" His response (paraphrased) was, "I never had 200 failures in my life. My family didn't think in terms of failure. They taught in terms of experiences and what could be learned. I just made my 201st discovery. I couldn't have made it without learning from the previous 200 experiences."

Another way to encourage young people is to take time to celebrate genuine successes with them. It is always easier to focus on the one F in a report card than on the five B's. Yes, you have to deal with the F's in a child's life. However, when you focus on the negative, or negate the positive with a "*but ...* you could have done better if ..." you give them a message that doing well is a waste of time because it won't be noticed. It illustrates the adage: whatever you focus on is what grows.

Encouragement is always more powerful when it is specific. Rather than simply praising a child's achievement or effort on a project or event, practice expressing exactly why you feel their achievement or effort is worth the encouragement.

In the long run, if your children know that you care and believe in them, the likelihood is high that they will eventually believe in themselves.

DAVID'S STORY: *THE VALUE OF MENTORS: "LEG-UP PEOPLE"*

I was 12 years old when I saved up enough money to buy my first horse. Actually, my dad paid half, but for $50 I got myself a retired packhorse named Caesar. All 17-hands and a six-inch protruding backbone was mine! I didn't have enough money for a saddle, so that first summer I learned to ride bareback. My grandpa used to say it was the only way to learn. I had a piece of baler twine for a bit and some old leather straps for reins. That's all I needed to have the time of my life, as long as I could get on, and stay on, that big old horse.

Enter Norris. Norris lived in an old dirt-floor log cabin down the road. He didn't have a possession to his name, except for the shack that he lived in, an old bicycle, and a couple of horses. He worked for my parents off and on as a hired hand for years, fixing fences, gardening, and building a barn. Norris was my hero when I was twelve. It was Norris who taught me how to hang onto a horse with my knees, and how to become one with that horse while I was riding on its back. It was Norris who taught me how a short, awkward 12-year-old gets onto a 17-hand packhorse. At first, Norris got me to climb up on his leg and then jump from his knee onto the old gelding. Gradually, I strengthened my arms and developed a technique for climbing onto the horse by myself.

Thinking back now on that summer, I realize that Norris was my "leg-up" person. He was one of those people who comes along in your life and gives you an abundance of support, encouragement and validation. For him, it seemed as if this was no great challenge. He simply showed up and cared.

In David's book, *Simple Living in a Complex World*, he discusses giving a "leg-up" to a child. A "leg-up" person is someone who enters your life and gives you a boost, someone who gives you more affirmation, support, and encouragement than negative criticism.[2]

Note that a parent doesn't have to do all the encouragement. It's especially tough to be a "leg-up" person to a child when you also have to be the disciplinarian. As the saying goes, it really does take a village to raise a child. A "leg-up" person can be an aunt or uncle, a teacher or neighbor, a grandparent or just someone who cares. Kids can never have too many of those.

c. Build self-trust through self-affirmation.

The goal of accountable parenting is to have your children leave home with a sense of their own confidence and ability to trust themselves, with less dependence on others for approval, security, and well-being. You know you have achieved your goal when your children make the shift from *parent*-affirmation to *self*-affirmation, when they change from *compliance* or *defiance* of your wishes, to a sense of a deeper assurance from within themselves. The best way to help your children make this transition is through quality conversations with them. Conversations are a tool to foster self-trust in your child while decreasing their reliance on you, the parent.

Being a part of your child's successes and failures can come in a variety of forms: report cards, performance in a sporting event, accomplishing chores or tasks around the house, or an expression in the performing arts. Rather than succumbing to the initial urge to praise or reprimand your kids, try taking time to explore with them first how *they* felt about their accomplishments, their perceived failures, and what they learned from the experience. Rather than laying your judgments and opinions onto their experience, try spending time exploring with them the perception *they* have of the incident and ways they can apply their learning in the future. Even though your opinion can be offered at some time in the conversation, remind them that even though you may be either proud or worried about them, what matters most is *what they think of themselves*. This is ultimately where you want them to arrive in life: more trusting of themselves and less in need of the approval of others, including yours as their parent, for their worth.

---

[2]For a more in-depth understanding of "leg-up" people in your child's life, see David Irvine's book, *Simple Living in a Complex World: Balancing Life's Achievements*, TO, Canada: Wiley & Sons, 2004.

PRINCIPLE THREE. Implement scheduled processes to create a strong and accountable family.

a. Create meaningful rituals in your family.

Rituals are practices that were originally designed to create connections between and within people in a community. As life has become more demanding and hectic, western society has often lost connection with the power of ritual. Many families never eat together any more, or when they do, they sit in front of a television. In many homes, there is never a time to sit and engage in meaningful dialogue. Often there are few activities that are done routinely as a family. Returning to family rituals can be a powerful way of unplugging from the frantic pace of modern life and regaining perspective. Rituals are not meant to be rigid, but are habits established in the home that take you away from the frenzied world and bring you into contact with your children, reminding you of your highest priorities.

Here is a list of rituals you may want to try integrating into your family life:

> ➢ Have a regular meal at least once a day where you "break bread together," and engage in meaningful dialogue about your day;
> ➢ Have a weekly "family council" meeting, where you create a structure for checking in and sharing together, where you discuss people's feelings, needs, and dreams;
> ➢ Read to your children before bedtime;
> ➢ Have a weekly "date" with each of your children, where you engage one-on-one in an activity you both enjoy;
> ➢ Attend church or a spiritual community together regularly.

b. Hold weekly accountability sessions to organize household chores.

Chores are not only a part of every family's life, they are a great tool for fostering accountability. They can also be your biggest battleground if they are not dealt with effectively. Begin the management of chores with a brainstormed list of every responsibility that is required for your family to function smoothly. List *everything*, from taking out the garbage to cooking supper to paying the bills. In order to learn to be accountable, it helps if children understand what it actually takes to run a household. Then, beside every chore, write the name of a person who will be accountable for that chore. It is best when people volunteer, but as a leader in your home, you

SUSAN LEVIN, OUR EDITOR, HAS A STORY ABOUT KIDDUSH:
A WEEKLY CONNECTION WITH FAMILY

Many Jewish families celebrate Kiddush, a Friday evening celebration of the commencement of the Sabbath, or day of rest. The central components of Kiddush are three blessings: for the lighting of the candles, for the wine, and for the *challah*, or holy bread. In addition to these traditional prayers, many Jewish families choose to supplement the ceremony with their own prayers or readings. In my home growing up, every Friday night, after blessings were sung, each family member would offer two lists. The first was a list of blessings from the week that had just gone by for which that person was particularly grateful, and the second was a list of challenges expected in the week ahead for which that person was praying for strength from God. When I got married, my husband and I continued this tradition and had our own weekly Kiddush. When we had our own children, we introduced them to the ritual.

For us, Kiddush is a time to come together as a family, to focus on blessings and challenges, and to share what is going on inside. One of the very important things we have learned is to stay consistent with it. To be honest, some weeks we don't do Kiddush. We're too tired, or we're lazy, or we're out somewhere. But that's really okay, because we always come back to it. It's not about doing the ritual perfectly; it's about appreciating its value when we have it, and stopping life for a moment, on a regular basis, to reflect and pray together.

At a recent Kiddush, we were going around the family circle and sharing what we were grateful for. Suddenly my son Ben, who is five, yelled out, "Mommy, is grateful your 'happy word'?" I said, "Well yes, Ben, I suppose it is!"

Now every Kiddush since that night, we share our "happy words." Often my husband and I say our happy words are "family," or "love," or "home." The children's happy words are much more interesting, such as "turkey burger," "mommydaddybenalina," or "nighnighwithmommy." Our Kiddush ritual is an evolving experience, a work in progress. There is no right or wrong way to do it. The important thing is that we do it.

are responsible to see that every chore is assigned to someone, and that there is an equal distribution depending on your children's ages and capabilities. Many chores, such as cleaning toilets, vacuuming, or preparing meals will, no doubt, need to be rotated. Some chores, such as meal clean-up, may have everyone's name listed.

As you write down names beside each chore, you can negotiate consequences for accomplishing or neglecting these chores and possibly work out formal accountability agreements such as those discussed in the following chapter. Finally, it is important to monitor, on a regular basis (through weekly family councils, for example) how well each person (including the parents!) is achieving his or her accountabilities.

c. Go beyond chores to *contribution*.

The need to be needed, to make an impact, and to be noticed lies at the root of being accountable. In previous generations, children were needed for a family to survive. They knew that they were important to the family and to the community. They knew they made a difference. For example, if you didn't milk the cows or tend to the growing of vegetables, you didn't eat. The line between work and making a difference was clearly drawn. There was no way to fake being needed. It was right in front of you.

While chores are always going to be a part of family life, *contributions* are different. Contribution is about making a meaningful difference. Chores take on a new meaning when the tasks are experienced as contributions to the family system. If you have ever done a cleaning project with a three-year-old, you know that they do not have to be persuaded or given incentives. Managed, yes, but they seem to come inherently motivated, with an innate desire to want to "help," to make a contribution.

It often takes much less time to vacuum a house or make supper or do the gardening if you do it yourself. Even though it is unrealistic to expect that children will help you with every responsibility in the home, the sure way to drain all motivation out of children is do everything for them for the first 10 years of their lives and then wonder when they reach adolescence, why they are no longer enthused about doing much around the house.

What we have learned is that you can't foster accountability in children by doing things *for* them. For children to become accountable, you have to create an environment where children can make a meaningful contribution.

Unfortunately, time and technology are two barriers to creating these kinds of environments in our modern, fast-paced world.

Families today face two significant challenges in the fostering of accountability through contribution. The first of these is a lack of *time*. Any parent understands that it takes much longer to bake a cake when your four-year-old is "helping" than to just do it yourself. While it would be unrealistic to invite each of your children to contribute to every household project, to foster a sense of being needed it is important to create some room, in this time-pressed society, to s-l-o-w d-o-w-n, step back, and allow your kids the space to contribute in their own, unique and awkward way.

The second challenge in fostering accountability in children through contribution is increased *technology*. Today we have a myriad of machines and equipment—from dishwashers and vacuum cleaners to calculators and computers—that create obviously more comfort and convenience in our lives but potentially absolve children of the responsibilities they once had when these technologies were not available, thus removing a child's sense of contribution that comes from being needed. As parents, we must be mindful of the role that technology can play in diminishing accountability in children, and carefully explore ways all family members can still feel needed. Just because technology is there to do the work, doesn't mean children aren't still needed! Children, to be accountable, need to learn to make the shift from being *consumers* (defined by Oxford as "destroying, squandering, using up") to genuine *contributors* ("building, serving, making better"). In a so-called "consumer society," making this shift is not just good for children; it's good for the culture.

If a child has a unique gift that can enrich the home, that child will learn the value of contribution. A child with a musical gift contributes to the family by the expression of that gift. A teenager who has a gift for mathematics might be able to assist with the family bookkeeping. Perhaps you have a young person in your home who is naturally mechanically-inclined and can help you fix things. Whenever your child teaches you something she learned in school she has contributed to you. We need to be very creative in ensuring that every child knows that the household is a better place because of his or her unique and special contribution.

PRINCIPLE FOUR. Balance "rights" with "accountabilities."

Throughout David's life, his parents stressed that as vital as human rights are in the development of a civil society, each of these rights must be accompanied by an accountability, an obligation or duty to that society and culture. When he was a teenager, David's family drafted a Family Charter of Rights and Freedoms with an accompanying Charter of Accountabilities. Below is part of the actual document that was developed in his home. Even though you may not agree with everything on this list, if the list inspires you, we invite you to develop your own. Like all documents of this nature, the power of this agreement is not in the words, it is in the *dialogue* the words engender and in the *ownership* of its contents by respective family members. The words are merely tools.

A FAMILY CHARTER OF RIGHTS AND FREEDOMS	CHARTER OF ACCOMPANYING ACCOUNTABILITIES
▪ to disagree	▪ to do so respectfully, and then get your chores done
▪ to wear designer clothes	▪ to pay for them yourself ("It's our job to cover your rear end, not decorate it!")
▪ to expect clean clothes	▪ to wash them, for yourself and others
▪ to negotiate curfews	▪ to be in when you say you will be in
▪ to decide our own bedtime	▪ to get yourself to school on time, keep up with your school assign ments and act humanely to others the next day
▪ to borrow the car	▪ to bring it back with more gas, cleaner, and in better shape than when you took it

NOTE: The children's list is on the left, the parents' on the right.

We have facilitated the process of identifying rights and accompanying accountabilities in schools, where a charter of rights and accountabilities was written for teachers, students, parents, and educational stakeholders, and developed with ownership and input from all four groups. We have also used this process in organizations and community associations, where stakeholder groups clarify and express their rights and accompanying accountabilities to each other. Through the heartfelt dialogues that result from these agreements, cultures begin to shift toward deeper reflective action and accountability.

PRINCIPLE FIVE. Teach your children about limits.

If you want your children to move past their own limitations, the first step is to teach them about limits. All privileges—e.g., the amount of television you allow them to watch, how late they are allowed to stay out, the time they spend with their friends, the money you spend on their college education, how long they can live at home—have limits. One of the advantages to living in a family with a lack of financial resources is that scarcity imposes its own boundaries.

The results of an environment where things come too easily are usually a lack of appreciation and resiliency. In an affluent society where so many people live on credit and in overdraft, how can children learn accountability? They won't if the goal of their caregivers is to make them happy. Everyone needs to know the difference between a *want* and a *need*, and everyone needs to know how to deal with not getting everything they want. They won't necessarily be happy about it, but giving them a taste of the real world while they are still young will help them grow into accountable adults.

Setting limits does not have to be done unilaterally. The best limits are established through open, respectful dialogue and negotiation with our children. Often, when we let them, young people are tougher on themselves than anyone else would be with them.

In order to set limits effectively, you need to have the courage and clarity to say "no" at times. This is where parents need support, either from a partner or a close network of friends. We could probably all learn to feel a little less sorry for our kids and bring a little more loving backbone into our homes. Our kids need it just as much as we do. Remember ... everything in balance.

Here are a few of the areas we invite you to consider in developing limits in your home:

> ➢ Limit, monitor, or stop altogether, watching television. Television can be a good tool for learning, but it is generally passive, lazy learning. Unless you are watching with them and discussing

what they are seeing, TV does little to promote relationships or accountability.

> Limit and monitor computer and technology use. Open dialogue is critical in this area. The most dangerous place for children these days is not in our neighborhoods. It is in front of a computer screen.

> Limit idle time. Put your children to work if they are bored.

> Limit the amount of money you spend on them and the things you buy them. Kids won't believe you that money really doesn't grow on trees. You have to show them.

> Limit the amount you spend on your child's post-secondary education. Of course we want our children to get a good education, but they won't appreciate things in the same way if everything is handed to them. Regardless of how many years of education beyond high school you are able or willing to pay for, draw a line where you feel it is right to do so.

> Start charging full market value for room and board if your children continue living at home after they have completed their education. Have the courage to evict them like any other landlord would if they don't meet their financial obligations. How can your children possibly develop the resources for surviving in the real world if living at home is not the real world?

> Consider carefully the amount of financial inheritance you are planning to leave your children. As our friend Don Campbell asks, "What would you rather leave your children: a rich financial inheritance with no character and values, or character and values with no money? With character and values we can create wealth and much more." Wealth without work can leave a dangerous legacy to our children: a lack of appreciation and an embedded sense of entitlement.

> Limit excessiveness in your own life. Be a power of example from whom your children can learn.

> Limit interruptions. Let the phone ring during supper hour and while making contact with your kids. If it's important, the person calling will call back.

> ### DAVID'S STORY: *CRACKING THE DEPENDENCY EGG*
>
> As a child on the farm, I remember watching our neighbor's chicks hatch. The chicks were pecking their way out of their shells, and in an effort to help them I cracked their eggs. To my astonishment, the chicks died. That day I learned a very important lesson the hard way: help isn't always helpful. Those chicks needed the struggle of hatching to survive and thrive. They needed to crack their own dependency eggs; they didn't need me to do it for them.

PRINCIPLE SIX. Don't be blinded by your children's pain.

Children will always bring problems and pain to you. Problems are a part of life, and it is not until we learn to trust ourselves that we will learn to live fully. Our ability to solve problems and handle the crises in our lives determines, to a large extent, the quality of our life. Your children's problems, whether in the classroom, playground, or backyard, are always learning opportunities for them—and for you. Sometimes the most challenging schoolteachers, the most difficult friends, and the darkest hours, are the greatest teachers, blessings in disguise, providing your children have a loving parent to walk them through such times, offering a supportive hand while guiding them to their own truth.

Attempting to protect children from failure and pain—to bubble wrap them—weakens them. Counselors at universities today will tell you of "helicopter parents" that "hover" over their college-age children, attempting to protect them from the pain of entering adulthood, and thereby robbing them of the strength they will need to deal with life. When a parent takes the time to lovingly guide children to their own solutions, those children learn to be extremely resourceful and develop a sense of strength in themselves.

PRINCIPLE SEVEN. Be a light, not a judge.

The goal of accountable parenting is to ignite—and subsequently unleash—your children's potential rather than to control and manipulate their development. From a small spark may burst a mighty flame. Igniting children's potential is like lighting one candle with another candle. Our flame as parents

SUSAN LEVIN, OUR EDITOR, HAS A STORY ABOUT HER DAUGHTER: IT MEANT A LOT TO ALINA.

Parenting teaches me all about accountability. I take my daughter, Alina, who is two years old, to a gymnastics class at the YMCA on Friday mornings. This past Thursday night, as I was rocking her to sleep in her room, Alina asked me, "Mommy, where am I going tomorrow?" I responded, "To gymnastics." She then asked, "Are you taking me?" I answered, "Yes, baby, I am."

The next morning I woke up with a fierce headache, brought on by days of stressful life situations and what I think was a small virus. I really felt terrible. I immediately called a babysitter and asked her if she could take Alina to gymnastics that morning. She said it would be fine, no problem. I had a conference call scheduled for early in the morning, and throughout that call, all I could think of was how terrible I felt physically, and how even more terrible I felt mentally, because I knew Alina would be really disappointed when she found out the babysitter, and not I, would be taking her to her class that morning. It suddenly occurred to me that I was being unaccountable. I had made Alina a promise. I was breaking that promise because I didn't feel well. When I considered my decision not to go in that light, I realized I was making a mistake, and that it was a serious one. Sure, I was tired, my head hurt, and I didn't feel like going. But I had made a promise, and barring a fever or a broken leg, I needed to show up for my daughter. I needed to be an accountable mom.

After my conference call ended, I went and found my daughter. She leaped out of her chair and ran to me, her face exploding in smiles. "Are you coming, Mommy?" I sure was.

can light up the life of every child with whom we connect while never weakening itself; the most important way to influence a child is through the power of *your* example.

Developing accountability in children is better *caught* than it is *taught*. Your actions will always speak louder than your lectures, as no one watches you more closely than your children. Stop and take a careful inventory: Do your children see you blaming and complaining or do they see you consistently taking ownership for your life? Do they watch you gossiping or do they see you practicing loyalty to others in their absence? In your free time, do your children see you spending hours in front of the television or do they see you spending your free time having stimulating conversations, exercising, contributing to others, relaxing in a healthy way, or pursuing outdoor activities? Do your children see you keeping promises—to yourself and others? Do they see you living within your means of income? In short, do your children see you living accountably?

Accountable parenting does not require perfection or sainthood (either real or feigned!). It requires self-honesty and an openness to discuss inconsistencies in the spirit of respect and renewed commitment. The power of leadership in your home lies not in your position but in your *presence*. Great parenting, like all great leadership, cannot be reduced to technique; great parenting comes from the *character*, the *identity*, and the *integrity* of the parent. Before judging your kids, take a look in the mirror.

PRINCIPLE EIGHT. Maintain perspective.

> *The children of today now love luxury. They have bad manners,*
> *and contempt for authority; they show disrespect for adults and love*
> *to talk rather than work or exercise. They contradict their parents,*
> *chatter in front of company, gobble down food at the table, and*
> *intimidate their teachers.*
> —SOCRATES, 489–399 B.C.

Socrates reminds us that every generation has struggled and continues to struggle with helping their children live accountably. We hope to continue to struggle, for perhaps it's only when we stop struggling that we fail. We're likely never going to get this parenting thing completely right. Maybe the real goal of parenting is to *enjoy* it more by trusting more in our children and their remarkable and unique journeys. Frankly, our suggestions in this chapter are as much for your benefit as parents as they are for your children.

Have you ever met an incompetent parent who was enjoying parenting? We doubt it. Accountable parenting as we have laid it out through our suggestions—spending more time with your kids, getting to know them, inviting dialogue through sharing, learning together, developing a sense of contribution, not getting sucked in to their pain, and setting clearer limits and boundaries—is a path to greater enjoyment as parents.

In the hustle and bustle of our busy lives, many parents of grown children will remind you, "The time went by so quickly. They grow up so fast." Take time to enjoy your kids, while you can.

PRINCIPLE NINE. Let go.

> *Your children are not your children.*
> *They are the sons and daughters of Life's longing for itself.*
> *They come through you but not from you,*
> *And though they are with you yet they belong not to you.*
> *You may give them your love but not your thoughts,*
> *For they have their own thoughts.*
> *You may house their bodies but not their souls.*
> *For their souls dwell in the house of tomorrow,*
> *Which you cannot visit, not even in your dreams.*
> *You may strive to be like them,*
> *But seek not to make them like you.*
> *For life goes not backwards, nor tarries with yesterday.*
>
> —KAHLIL GIBRAN

Accountable parenting is about learning to love, and then spending the rest of our lives letting go, realizing that our children are not our children. Parenting is a lot like gardening. No plants ever grew because you commanded that they do so or because you threatened them. Plants, like human beings, will only grow in the appropriate conditions, when they are given proper care, love, and nourishment. Finding the desirable environment and sustenance for plants—and people—is a matter of continual enquiry, awareness, and investment. As gardeners of your children's souls, remember, despite your best efforts, children must find and grow their own roots in their own way. Gardening has much to do with the culture of the garden, and less to do with the outcome. Each child has their own spirit and must, eventually, find their own path, their own unique expression of that essence. The very best we can do, as the gardeners of our family, is to create the culture and leave the outcome to a higher power.

Perhaps the best way to summarize our philosophy of parenting and fostering accountability in our homes is to share a quote from David's mother, found in her journal after her death. We hope it will inspire you in the most important leadership role in life: developing accountable, authentic young people.

Every parent, no matter how hard they try, will be both a blessing and a curse to their children. My hope is that my children will appreciate the "blessing," if not immediately then later in life, and perhaps more importantly that they will take the "curse" and, like an oyster irritated by a grain of sand, over time use it as a catalyst to build layers of character and understanding—thus producing a pearl.

—JOYCE IRVINE

CHAPTER 7

WRITING AN AUTHENTIC ACCOUNTABILITY AGREEMENT™

B Y NOW YOU UNDERSTAND THAT ACCOUNTABILITY is an attitude, a mindset, a decision to be counted on, and that an accountable culture—whether an organization, family, or community—begins with you. However, when you work and live with people, you have expectations of each other, and just *living* accountably isn't enough. Sometimes you need the further clarity and accountability that formal written agreements can provide. Structured agreements can be helpful in any relationship where specific results are expected: performance management in your workplace, volunteer coordination in a community association, administration of household chores in a family, carrying out a job interview, clarifying a new role at work, or persuading children to take responsibility for their chores without having to be reminded. This chapter outlines some key elements for writing and using agreements with precision and commitment, agreements that define and clarify expectations, promises, accountabilities, and consequences.

An accountability agreement is a brief document that outlines your vision and personal contribution in your current role, along with clearly defined parameters of that role, personal promises, requests for support, consequences, and plans for keeping the agreement active. The agreement can be personal (within yourself) or interpersonal, (between two or more parties).

Before getting into the nuts and bolts of an actual agreement, two vital points are worth emphasizing. First, no document can serve as a substitute for leadership. No document will make a real difference in organizations or in people's lives where leadership and commitment are lacking. As we discussed in Chapter 1, no document, in itself, can create accountability. Our goal is to invite you to write and use these agreements if and when you need them, and also recognize that some organizations and people are better suited to working with these types of agreements than others. If an organization's members are apathetic or controlling, or if a person involved in the situation is immature or overly dependent, any document will fall flat. There are no shortcuts to commitment and no substitutes for meaningful and respectful conversation or leadership. People need to be informed and involved, their input needs to carry influence, and they must have the right to choose for themselves. This is not a tool to turn unaccountable people into accountable people. It is not a club with which to punish, control, or coerce others, or a program where people must commit to agreements with which they are uncomfortable. Using accountability agreements in these ways would, in fact, be counter to the very reason for taking the personal initiative to be more accountable. This being said, many organizations have found a way to replace job descriptions and performance reviews with this process in a respectful and meaningful way.

The other point we wish to stress is that even if you want to increase your accountability by taking time to create and implement an accountability agreement, you don't need a document for you to be accountable. While writing agreements down will help clarify expectations, we have met many accountable people who have integrity and yet do not use any kind of written agreement to clarify expectations, promises, or consequences. They apply all the elements of this suggested agreement format without actually writing them down. It just seems to come naturally to them.

Between us, we have been learning and applying principles of accountability to organizations for more than 40 years. Below are five key elements we have found to be valuable in creating powerful and meaningful accountability agreements.[1] Feel free to adapt these elements as needed to make *your* agreement process meaningful for your unique situation.

---

[1] We give tribute to our original template for writing Accountability Agreements to the original developers, Bruce Klatt, Shaun Murphy, and David Irvine. This template can be found in *Accountability: Getting a Grip on Results*, Bow River Press, Calgary, AB, Canada, 2004. See also, *Aligned Like A Laser: Achieving Organizational Alignment Through Clear Accountabilities for Results*, by Bruce Klatt and Shaun Murphy, Bow River Press, Calgary, AB, Canada, 2004.

FIVE KEY ELEMENTS OF THE AUTHENTIC ACCOUNTABILITY AGREEMENT: *IN BRIEF*

Element One. Contribution Statement: What is the higher purpose of your role—how does it connect to the "big picture" of your current organization and your life?" What value do you bring to your organization? What is your "business within the business?"

Element Two. Accountabilities: What specific deliverables are you personally responsible for?

Element Three. Support Requirements: What accountabilities do you require of others so that you can accomplish yours?

Element Four. Consequences: What happens if your accountabilities are/are not achieved?

Element Five. Follow up: How will this agreement be maintained?

FIVE KEY ELEMENTS OF THE AUTHENTIC ACCOUNTABILITY AGREEMENT: *DISCUSSION*

ELEMENT ONE. Contribution Statement

For the past decade, we have become increasingly disappointed with traditional performance programs inside organizations that have been forced upon people in an archaic command-and-control, patriarchal approach to accountability, and where accountability has been diminished to a drive for detail and the measurement of exact results for the purpose of fault-finding. Accountability is a critical component of organizational life, but so is survival. Unleashing the potential of your organization and the people within it is far more important than some bureaucratic emphasis on "keeping people accountable." When people sign up willingly, accountability is effortless because it comes from *commitment*, rather than *compliance*. In fact, people will be the first to hold themselves accountable in a genuinely respectful environment.

Our intent, in this first element of an authentic accountability agreement is to re-imagine our working relationships in terms of a *covenant* rather than a *contract*, one that is built on meaningful personal internal consideration as well as on dialogue between yourself and those who depend on you. This covenant forms the foundation of a meaningful and shared commitment to a cause beyond self-interest, originating from an ongoing inquiry into your authentic self and the nature of your contribution to the world around you.

We learned years ago from Max Depree, the long-time chairman and CEO of Herman Miller (one of the most innovative and admired companies in America), about the difference between a *strategy* and a *legacy*.[2] Max said that a strategic plan—understanding the value you provide to customers through your unique strengths—is necessary but not sufficient to the full task of leadership. Leaving a legacy—articulating and bringing to life the kind of organization or community that you want be a part of, or the kind of life you are committed to living, is very different.

Regardless of what you call this first element, it is the legacy component of personal and organizational leadership that Max is referring to. What matters is that you use this element to step out of your current role and examine carefully how it fits into the broader context of your life. It is a declaration of your accountability, a covenant to yourself and to those you serve, the legacy that you are committed to leave by the authentic life you are living.

We invite you to consider the following areas under this first element:

➤ What gives you a sense of satisfaction and fulfillment?

➤ What brings you passion, energy, and meaning in your current role?

➤ What kind of a person do you want to be known as—and remembered for?

➤ What is the legacy you most desire to leave?

➤ What is your contribution, the highest value you bring to this organization/ relationship? How does this contribution connect to the organization's mission and vision? (If you were outsourced in this organization, and hired back as a private contractor, how would you describe the value that you bring?)

➤ How will you contribute to building a better culture here?

Reflecting on and writing a Contribution Statement is intended to give you a sense of why you are doing what you are doing. Thus, it is a potential source of energy. It is the passion missing in many traditional performance management processes. It ensures loyalty and commitment. The statement of contribution makes accountability agreements authentic. It gets to what's

---

[2]Depree, Max, *Leadership Jazz: The Art Of Conducting Business Through Leadership*, Followship, Teamwork, Touch, And Voice, New York, NY: Bantam Doubleday Dell Publishing Group, 1992.

in your heart. We will all leave a legacy. The Contribution Statement answers the question, *"What will yours be?"*

> Note: Articulating answers to these "contribution questions" can be valuable in a long-term relationship. However, this element may not be necessary in simple agreements with clearly-defined expectations and results, and you may choose not to use a Contribution Statement if it is not relevant for your agreement. For those interested in understanding the power of this element in an authentic accountability agreement, however, the following examples will be useful illustrations.

JIM'S STORY: *THE POWER OF AN EMPLOYEE'S CONTRIBUTION STATEMENT*

In the early days of Hewlett Packard, a customer was taken on a tour of the company's manufacturing plant by a plant manager in the medical instruments division. While walking through the facility, they passed by a small group of employees in the middle of a short stand-up meeting. The plant manager stopped to say hello to the employees, introduced the customer, and they all entered into a short discussion, during which the customer asked one of the employees what her job was. Without hesitation, she replied, "My job is to save babies' lives in the first few months of pregnancy."

After further conversation, the customer learned that this woman actually worked on an assembly line and her task was to stuff printed circuit boards that were used in fetal heart monitors sold around the world. But it made quite an impression on the customer to hear the assembly line worker describe her job in this way! Hearing these types of stories was a common experience at Hewlett Packard, and everyone who worked there took great pride in circulating them, as they were a source of inspiration throughout the company.

The following are samples of Contribution Statements that we have come across in our work. Note that it is not necessarily the words that make these meaningful to the writers. The inquiry and subsequent dialogue give them life—not the words on the paper.

Example One. An Architect.
When facilitating accountability agreements with an architectural firm, one of the founders, in his accountability agreement, came up with the following Contribution Statement:

> *My higher purpose is to gain personal well-being/fulfillment, to sustain a life full of imagination and discovery, by exploring, experiencing, and contributing to my physical, social, and cultural environments.*
>
> *To celebrate this transition period of my life through a balance of: increased wealth, professional maturity, reputation, creativity, leadership, fitness, travel, and personal time.*
>
> *Architecture involves the transformation of Nature into Culture for the purpose of creating artifacts and places that enable our engagement with existence in a meaningful, hopeful, and human way.*
>
> *"One minute in the life of the world is passing by. Paint it as it is" (Cezanne).*

When this partner read his statement to his senior management team, it was a significant emotional experience for every single person in the room. Reading this to his team inspired him to share some stories about what was behind the words. The entire experience evoked a depth and clarity about the passion behind his work and his commitment to building the culture. For him, architecture was a means to a much higher end. With his sharing, he inspired all of his leadership team to look more deeply within themselves and to bring more of their authentic selves, their ability to contribute in a unique way based on their unique talents, to the organization. Indeed, it initiated conversations within the firm that created lasting change in the culture.

Example Two. An Office Manager.
David once employed a 23-year-old office manager whose Contribution Statement outlined three deep commitments she brought to her work:

I want to be remembered as a person who changed the way David did his business.

I want to be known as a person who kept her word.

I want to be known as a person who brightened up the day of every person who called this office.

Through this woman's energy and passion, she did indeed change the way David did his business.

Further examples.
Here is a Contribution Statement of an HR manager:

My contribution as an organizational leader is to ensure that each and every employee's contribution to the business will improve this organization's image and impact, both internally and externally.

A secondary school teacher's Contribution Statement:

My promise to myself and to the students I serve is to create a class-room that ensures a stimulating, dynamic, shared learning environment that:
> *Engages my students.*
> *Respects the dignity and self-worth of everyone in the classroom.*
> *Engages parents, students, and teachers to work together as partners.*

The Contribution Statement of a founder of a family business in agriculture provided a clear statement of his intention and contribution to his ranch and to his successors:

My intention is to:
> *Use the ranch to help my children become mature, accountable adults.*
> *Step out of the management of the ranch and assist where I am asked.*
> *Develop my consulting business [with my wife].*
> *Let go, over time, of the ownership and leadership of the ranch.*

> ➤ *Be an employee on the ranch so I can be free to travel and consult [with my wife].*
> ➤ *Be prepared to step back into the management if my kids don't stick around. **There are no hidden agendas.***

DAVID'S STORY: *CLARIFYING NEEDS THROUGH A CONTRIBUTION STATEMENT*

Years ago, as I was building my speaking business, I was dumping far too much work on my amazing organizer and life partner, Val. At that time she was a stay-at-home household executive, administrator, marketer, and sales manager, all wrapped up in one complete package. After a night of writing up contracts until 2 a.m., she gracefully challenged me to practice what I was preaching and have us each write a clear accountability agreement. Her Contribution Statement at that time was as follows:

My contribution and commitment is to create a stable, supportive, loving home environment that will nurture and sustain productive, accountable, contributing citizens for the next generation.

I will work in partnership with David to provide the needed personal support to grow the business and the relationship.

After discussing this statement together, it became obvious that even though Val was *competent* in each of these responsibilities, she wasn't *passionate* about them. We needed to hire the staff to fill the gap that lay outside Val's desired contribution. But even more importantly, by spelling out a clear Contribution Statement for herself and seeing right in front of us the misalignment between her current job and her desired contribution, we developed a strategy for bringing her work into alignment with her authentic self. It wasn't so much the excess work that was stressing her. It was the *misalignment* between her work and her spirit.

A Contribution Statement is a great tool to assess your level of alignment between your current role and your deepest desires. Indeed, the accountability agreement process is intended to be instrumental in diminishing your stress level as well as amplifying your impact by helping you focus on creating successful outcomes that are in alignment with your authentic self.

We conclude this section on Contribution Statements with a quote by Gary Zukav, who articulates beautifully what it feels like to discover this alignment between your work and your soul:[3]

> *"When the deepest part of you becomes engaged in what you are doing ... when what you do serves both yourself and others, when you do not tire on the inside ... but seek the **sweet satisfaction** of your life and your work. What then?*
>
> *Then you know you are doing what you are meant to be doing."*

ELEMENT TWO. Accountabilities

Accountabilities are your side of the agreement and are the promises that you make to the people who depend on you. They establish a clear understanding of and commitment to what is expected within a specific role. The purpose of this part of the accountability agreement is to clarify expectations. To do that, negotiate and quantify everything possible. All parties should be direct with their requirements, to ensure that their respective expectations are both realistic and workable for all.

There are two kinds of accountabilities; you may choose to implement either or both in your agreement:

1. **Operational Accountabilities** are brief, clear statements of the *results* you are promising to deliver; they describe what gets accomplished.
   a. What specific outcomes or results do you promise to deliver?
   b. What accountabilities are uniquely your own at your level of the organization?
2. **Leadership Accountabilities** are a description, also expressed in outcomes, of the work environment—the culture—that you are accountable to create in order to make exceptional performance and greatness possible.

---

[3]Gary Zukav, *The Seat Of The Soul*, Simon & Schuster Publishers, New York, NY., 1989, p. 236.

A LIST OF SOME OF DAVID'S ACCOUNTABILITIES AS PRESIDENT AND CEO OF AN INTERNATIONAL SPEAKING AND CONSULTING COMPANY.
(For brevity's sake, and because goals tend to be fluid, some goals are not included in this excerpt.)

Operational Accountabilities:

- A financially and spiritually viable and sustainable business that will support us in our dreams and desired Quality Of Life
- Expectations of every client exceeded
- Continual marketing opportunities that exceed the expectation of all staff
- Updated intellectual capital that continuously brings renewed value to our clients

How we measure operational accountabilities:

- Level of income
- Feedback from clients after events
- Number of leads that David brings to his sales team after events
- Feedback in weekly team meetings

Leadership Accountabilities:

- A "generosity of spirit" in all our relationships
- The success of everyone on our team
- A safe working environment where risk-taking and failures equal learning opportunities
- A positive, effective, and value-added relationship with all our staff and stakeholders
- My own development and well-being—personally and professionally; I will come to work mentally, physically, and spiritually fresh

How we measure leadership accountabilities:

- Ongoing feedback from, and conversations with, staff, partners, and family members; personal reflection

---

HERE IS A LIST OF DAVID'S SALES MANAGER'S ACCOUNTABILITIES:

Operational Accountabilities:

- Ensure a viable business through the attainment of all my sales goals (measured by number of sales made and income from sales)
- Fee integrity is maintained on all contracts (measured by consistency of financial value received from clients)
- All client expectations are exceeded (measured by post-event feedback administered by David)
- Free up David's time to enable him to do what he does best by managing all aspects of sales (measured by feedback from David)

Leadership Accountabilities

- Positive energy that builds and fosters positive, value-added relationships with every one of our stakeholders (measured by feedback from stakeholders, especially clients)
- Solution-oriented environment (measured by feedback from clients and stakeholders)
- I will remain on David's list of people to count on (measured by feedback from David)
- Openness to learn and offer perspective (measured by feedback from David)

---

a. For both the operational and leadership accountabilities we suggest assigning a *measurement*. *Measurements* are descriptions of how and when you will meaningfully assess, quantify and measure how successful you have been in fulfilling the results you are accountable for. Measurements list the different ways to assess your success, with respect to each of your accountabilities. They are the indicators that you are achieving, or not achieving, your results.

b. Within each of these accountabilities are specific, short-term *goals* (usually 60 to 90 days) that will take you toward the achievement of your accountabilities. Accountabilities set the context for goal setting. Goals are measurable or observable results that you promise to accomplish within a given time period. We recommend that you have at least one short-term goal for every accountability.

ELEMENT THREE. Support Requirements

Support requirements are the accountabilities you require from others to ensure that you will have the support necessary to fulfill your own accountabilities and goals. Just as accountabilities are listed in results language, so, too, are support requirements. Every support requirement has a name attached to it and a request for a specific accountability. This is what locks people into an accountable relationship. Your requests for support will be on someone's accountability agreement, just as others' needs for your support will be on your accountability agreement.

SUPPORTS REQUESTED OF DAVID IN HIS SALES MANAGER'S ACCOUNTABILITY AGREEMENT:

- Audiences receive value that exceeds their expectations in all engagements (as measured by evaluation ratings)
- An influx of continual marketing opportunities (as measured, in part, by the number of leads brought back from engagements)
- Sales training and coaching (as measured in a specific budget expectation for training, coaching, and annual development opportunities related to bettering herself in the business)
- Know David's business and message (as measured by reimbursement of travel costs to attend some of David's events)

ELEMENT FOUR. Consequences

This section describes the consequences regarding what you would like from your organization in return for delivering on your accountabilities. They are a statement of what is important to you, considering what is fair and reasonable within your current environment. There are few better ways to get to know a person—what motivates them and what matters to them—than discussing and negotiating consequences. Although an accountability agreement is often made more powerful by being made public, consequences are normally kept confidential.

To assess consequences, consider the following questions:

➤ What are you hoping to gain from fulfilling your part of the agreement?

➤ What recognition is important to you?

➤ How do you want to be recognized?

➤ What is reasonable and respectable?

DAVID'S STORY: *POSITIVE CONSEQUENCES FROM PEOPLE-BASED VALUES.*

A few years ago, David's sale's manager expressed a desire to move from Alberta to a city on Vancouver Island. She always wanted to return to the ocean, to be closer to her parents and son, and to enjoy the quality of life that the community on the coast offered her. They negotiated carefully how she could continue to produce the results for which she was accountable and live on the west coast. All parties experienced positive consequences. She was able to live in the place that supported her authentic self, and the business grew and cemented its relationship with a very loyal and accountable employee.

Following are the negotiated consequences of an HR Manager:

➤ Financial reward arrangements as negotiated

➤ Continued and increased responsibilities beyond Human Resources

➤ A larger role in employee town halls, investor meetings, and community events representing our company

➤ Executive Human Resources/Public Sector Relations program in the coming year

➢ Consideration for a senior vice-president operating role in two to three years

➢ The opportunity to act in a senior vice-president operating role in an extended absence situation

These are the consequences of a senior vice-president in the hospitality industry:

➢ Competitive compensation, benefits, and short-term incentive programs

➢ Increased availability of stock options

➢ More opportunity to enjoy success with stakeholders, family and friends

If you are employed in public service or in a large bureaucracy, your options for consequences are obviously going to be different than in a small entrepreneurial business. The most meaningful consequences for accountable people, regardless of position, are internal, such as personal satisfaction and fulfillment in your work. However, there are a few areas that may be up for negotiation with your boss, such as:

➢ Increased flex time

➢ Contract renewal

➢ Development/training opportunities, including specific conferences you would like to attend

➢ Promotions

➢ Horizontal moves

We have observed that negotiating these types of innovative consequences is very appealing to the younger work force. Negotiating consequences has also proven strategic in retaining employees, as they feel they have far more influence on their own lives through the process.

ELEMENT FIVE. Follow up

Follow up is a statement that indicates how your agreement will be maintained as a meaningful and flexible document over time, a true work in progress. When discussing your accountability agreement with those you are accountable to, it is critical to negotiate how often you will need to review your accountability agreement and with whom. For this element, consider the following questions:

> How will you keep this agreement current and ensure it is a "living" document?
> How will you hold yourself accountable?
> How will others hold you accountable?
> How often will you review it? With whom?

Getting Started: Six Steps ...

As with anything new, the hardest part is getting started. Your appreciation for the depth and power of Authentic Accountability Agreements™ will grow only as you begin to apply these ideas. The magic happens when you start following these steps. You don't have to get these perfect. The learning will be in the doing.

Step 1. Start with you. Don't wait for permission to be more strategic and valuable. When you are ready to sit and write a first draft of your own accountability agreement, be prepared to spend two to three hours in a quiet place away from your usual work area. You may want to bring along any available documentation that describes your role (old job descriptions, core competency profiles, etc.), or statements of your department's purpose, goals and strategies; these may be helpful as references.

We recommend that you keep your agreement brief (less than two pages if possible). Use terminology and headings that are important to you and understandable to others. Make it your own. The terms we use are simply guidelines, not rules. Making them meaningful to you is what will make these agreements authentic and effective.

If you want others around you to draft their own agreements, inspire them through your example. Your excitement and enthusiasm about the impact the agreement can have on your life and work will be contagious. Let others witness the changes in you and they will choose to follow suit.

Step 2. Find a mentor. You will be most effective if you can involve at least one other person who is familiar with your role, understands your goals, and has the willingness to invest energy in challenging and supporting you. If you find yourself writing your agreement and all you are doing is describing your role (as though this is just another "job description"), you have not gone far enough. After completing the agreement, the goal is to have a "Wow!" feeling that comes from reframing your role and seeing it with brand new eyes and brand new possibilities. A mentor can be helpful to challenge you to find a new perspective.

Step 3. Negotiate with your positional leader. Take the first draft of your accountability agreement to the person(s) to whom you are accountable. Go through each part of the agreement that you are willing to share. Be open for feedback, suggestions, and requests. Remember, they have the final say when it comes to accountability in your organization. And *you* have the final say when it comes to accountability in your life.

Continue to rewrite your agreement until you both agree on what is written. The more you can negotiate for results and clarify the parameters of both parties' expectations, the more likely you will be to establish the trust and support necessary to fulfill the agreement's promises.

Step 4. Share your agreement with your direct reports—those you serve. Once you have acceptance and support from the person or people to whom you are accountable, you are ready to take your agreement to your direct reports. (If you have no direct reports, consider sharing it with your customers, clients, and people you serve.) Share the insights you gained from going through the experience as well as the content of your agreement. Meet individually with those whose names appear on your support requirements, negotiate your needs for support, and ensure that they are committed to providing the support requested.

With the exception of your negotiated consequences, which you may decide to keep confidential, we suggest you make your agreement public. We have seen many people hang their agreements in their offices.

Step 5. Make connections with other accountable people. Although you are welcome to invite anyone who reports to you to write their agreement, you may want to pick two or three allies—accountable, strategic leaders on your team—and invite them personally to write their own agreements. Offer your personal support and coaching to these people. Discuss ways you can spread the power of this agreement throughout your culture. Use their support as a power of example.

Step 6. Monitor success. There are four primary goals for writing agreements. Ask yourself, periodically, if you are achieving these goals. Does your agreement:

(a) *create clarity about your role and direction?* As we discussed earlier, taking agreements out of your head and putting them down on paper frees up more of your creative energy to focus on real priorities, instead of worrying or wondering about what you have promised. We have discovered that one of the most effective characteristics of a great leader is the capacity to be clear about expectations. Many people are frustrated in their current roles because they are unclear about the expectations that others have of them. Thus, they are left guessing.

(b) *create conversation at a new depth, with the right focus?* The power and meaning of these agreements lies not in the words, but rather in the conversation that the words help you create, both within yourself and within the lives of people that matter to you.

(c) *create energy to live your passion and highest aspirations in what you are doing?* If these agreements seem to be just another "make-work project" or a "command performance," and if you are not finding yourself engaged and energized by doing them, then either find a new way of doing them or set them aside and do something more important. These agreements are meant to bring life into your role, not diminish it.

(d) *create new awareness in your current roles and in your life?* These elements for creating a powerful and effective accountability agreement are meant to help you grow and develop, both in your work and in your life. They are not a club with which to beat up yourself or anyone else. The agreement is a tool to help you better understand yourself and reveal new possibilities.

Alternative Applications

Although accountability agreements are typically used within organizations, here are three accountability agreements in alternate environments to illustrate their broad application and potential. As you read through these, be aware that the power of these agreements is not in the words, but in the conversation and clarity that follows. The agreements themselves are always a means to a higher end.

EXAMPLE ONE:
AN ACCOUNTABILITY AGREEMENT BETWEEN DAVID'S DAUGHTER, HAYLEY, WHEN SHE WAS NINE YEARS OLD, IN PURSUIT OF GETTING A DOG FROM THE HUMANE SOCIETY

Contribution Statement:

I will take full responsibility for the care and safety of the dog in our home without having to be bugged.

List of Dog Promises (Accountabilities):

- Take for walks
- Buy treats with my own money
- Serve food
- Brush and bath
- Buy collar and leash with my own money
- If she gets lost, make lost dog posters
- Refill water when she needs it
- Pick-up doggie-doo
- Take dog to vet
- Do this without being bugged
- Ask parents early to join on walks
- Love her

Measurements:

- Talks with Dad and Mom
- How much I need to be reminded
- How mad Dad gets
- Dog "Report Card"
- The dog doesn't die

Goals:

- Feed every day and take for walks
- Give her a bath once a month or when she needs it
- Get an A on my Dog Report Card this month

Supports Needed:

- Take me to the Humane Society
- Money for food and brush
- Teach me how to look after her
- Drive us to the vet
- If she gets lost, help me find her
- Company for walks (remind me two hours ahead of time, if possible)
- Trust me to take care of her

Consequences:

If I show more accountability, I would like more freedom:

- Later bedtimes
- More sleepovers
- Friends over more often
- Increased self-respect

Follow Up:

- This agreement will be posted on the fridge where we can all refer to it as needed
- We will discuss our progress in our weekly family counsel meetings
- Dog Report Card will be discussed at our family counsel meeting once a month

EXAMPLE TWO
AN ACCOUNTABILITY AGREEMENT BETWEEN DAVID AND VAL AND THEIR DAUGHTER CHANDRA'S ELEMENTARY SCHOOL TEACHER

Parents' Contribution Statement

Our contribution as parents is to ensure that Chandra is a responsible, contributing citizen who experiences joy in learning and in living.

Accountabilities:

We, as parents, are personally accountable for ensuring that:

- Chandra comes to school with a sense of joy and responsibility for herself and her own learning.
- Chandra has an understanding that education is more than going to school.
- Mme Séguin feels that her commitment to Chandra's learning is supported by us as parents (e.g., regular monthly participation in the classroom, enthusiastic participation in special school events with Chandra, commitment/involvement in student-led conferences).
- Chandra comes to the classroom *learning ready* (e.g., she is excited about learning and about school, she brings a positive attitude to the classroom, she is rested, nourished and emotionally supported).
- Chandra takes responsibility for completing all her assignments and meeting deadlines outlined by Mme Séguin.

Measures:

- One-on-one dialogue (e.g., in student-led conferences, but also other times as needed)
- Chandra's attitude toward school and Mme Séguin as measured through parental observations and conversations
- Observation of the classroom
- Mme Séguin's observation and feedback about Chandra
- Our relationship (as Chandra's parents) with Mme Séguin
- Report cards

Goals:

- Chandra is seen by her teacher as having a superb relationship with Mme Séguin and with her classmates.
- Chandra exceeds all requirements set out by the department of education for this grade level in French Immersion.
- Chandra is seen as a student who initiates her own learning.
- Chandra is viewed as taking a leadership role in school-based extra-curricular activities.

Support Agreement:

From Mme Séguin

- Continue to do a superb job of relating, encouraging, and teaching our daughter.
- Continue to come to the classroom refreshed and ready to teach.
- Openness and honesty about Chandra's progress with Chandra and with us as parents (e.g., regular progress reports—verbal or written).
- Providing Chandra with an education experience that fits her capabilities (e.g., age appropriate learning resources).

From the Principal

- Continue to support Mme Séguin and us, as Chandra's parents, in our efforts to ensure Chandra's success at school.

Consequences:

When we achieve our goals and accountabilities:

- Chandra will be excited to go to school (most days) and enjoy the learning process.
- Mme Séguin will enjoy Chandra's presence in the classroom and feel a sense of accomplishment in Chandra's success.
- Val and David will have a great relationship with Mme Séguin and will continue to speak highly of her as a dedicated professional.
- Val and David will be proud of Chandra and the school she attends.

Follow up:

- We will review this document in conjunction with each student led conference (three times/year).
- Val and David will meet with Mme Séguin as needed to discuss our progress as partners in the education process.

EXAMPLE THREE
AN ACCOUNTABILITY AGREEMENT FOR A YOUNG ADULT JOB SEEKER

The following is a unique application of this tool, written by David's daughter, Mellissa, when she was 18 years old, in her application for a summer job after completing high school. It is an excellent statement of personal promise to a prospective employer. Note that the more you research an organization, the more powerful you can make your agreement to your potential employer by clarifying the value that you will bring to them.

In this example, Mellissa decided to have both a Higher Purpose Statement as well as a Contribution Statement.

If you have ever been in a position of hiring someone, visualize your reaction to receiving a resumé or covering letter with the following included:

Higher Purpose Statement

My life, as I see it at this point, is about being an artist, and expressing my artistic gifts. This job will give me a great opportunity to develop my craft and express these gifts in the service of your customers. I want to express my passions, serve others, and make a difference in the world.

Contribution Statement

I intend to add value and contribute to the profitability of my employer's company. I am personally committed to bringing a positive, self-responsible attitude to my work.

Accountabilities

I am personally accountable for:

- Being on time for work every day.
- Bringing a positive attitude to work every day.
- Fulfilling my accountabilities. (I am here to add value, not just put in time.)
- Being eager to learn and enhance my skills.
- Working in a cooperative manner with all employees.
- Serving the customer to the best of my ability.
- Being a hard-working, reliable, honest employee.

- Being creative and self-motivated.
- Working late, when needed, to achieve my accountabilities.

Measures

- Feedback from my employer.
- Feedback from customers.
- Feedback from co-workers.
- My personal sense of accomplishment and contribution.

Goals

- I want to learn more about customers and how to serve them better.
- I am very creative, and want to find a way to develop these skills in my work.
- I want to learn more about bookkeeping and accounting.
- I would like to work part-time once I return to school in September.

Supports

- My employer's trust in me, although I realize I must earn that trust.
- My employer's willingness to give me feedback as much as possible.
- My employer's patience, as I have lots to learn and may make mistakes once in a while.

Consequences

- I take personal satisfaction in knowing that I am doing a job to the best of my ability.
- My raises should be conditional on the value that I add to my employer's business.

Follow up

- I would like to meet regularly with my employer and/or my immediate supervisor to discuss my progress in relation to my accountabilities.
- I would like ongoing input on my performance in relation to my employer's expectations.

CHAPTER 8

CONCLUSION

FOLLOWING ONE OF OUR intensive authentic leadership retreats, a partic-ipant—an executive assistant to a CEO of a large firm—sat quietly after everyone had left and the room was empty. Sitting down beside her, we said, "You look thoughtful. Do you want to put words to your experience?" Here was her response.

"I was most intrigued by the notion that living accountably can affect virtually every aspect of one's life. I know now that accountability is not just a concept or a nice idea. I can see how accountability in life and at work is actually a force of life for individuals and groups. When you are impeccable about keeping promises to yourself and others, you have the capacity to change your life and the world around you. Accountability starts with *ownership*: honoring your own values. I'm not making changes in my life for my boss or my family or for anyone else. I'm doing this for me.

In addition, accountability is about building a foundation of strong *character*. As I reflect on what matters most to me, I know that I will follow-through with *courage* and *commitment* to live life in alignment with my voice and my values.

Finally, accountability is about *citizenship*, I used to think you had to have authority in order to be accountable. I know now that I can be account-able for building a healthy organization and community even though I do not control it."

This woman described and summarized the real power of our approach to leadership and life. Accountability is not just a process for managing expectations in your life; when applied on a daily basis, it's a philosophy that will transform your life. It's a foundation of living that truly enables greatness—the capacity to be all you can be—in every area of your life.

In this book, we have offered you many ideas about accountability. We have also presented you many actions—vehicles—through which you can explore bringing more accountability into your life. In our experience, the results of living accountably are well worth the endeavor.

You have probably noticed that we like lists. Our intent in writing lists is to make the information practical and readily accessible to action. Lists are also our way of highlighting our core messages from our pages of text.

In this final section, we conclude with one more list, a list of strategies to get to the heart of authentic accountability on a daily basis, guiding you to fully realize its power in your life. Whatever strategies from this list you choose to implement, as imperfect as your efforts may be, if your commitment is personal integrity and actions that are aligned with core values that reflect that integrity, you will no doubt find great reward through the bridges of trust that you build.

EIGHT STRATEGIES TO GET TO THE HEART OF AUTHENTIC ACCOUNTABILITY: *IN BRIEF*

Strategy One.   Seek Self-Awareness.

Strategy Two.   Maintain Attentiveness.

Strategy Three.   Find Solitude.

Strategy Four.   Seek Clarity.

Strategy Five.   Discover a Higher Purpose.

Strategy Six.   Commit to Service.

Strategy Seven.   Foster Community.

Strategy Eight.   Maintain Gratitude.

STRATEGY ONE. Seek Self-Awareness.

To be accountable you must be in touch with yourself. The quality of your work will always be intricately intertwined with the condition of your inner life. In order to maintain authentic accountability, make a commitment every day to use the experiences you have had and the people you have interacted with to evolve your awareness of who you are. If you have a strong emotional reaction to a person or circumstance (positive or negative), an opportunity has been presented for you to learn about yourself.

STRATEGY TWO. Maintain Attentiveness.

Be present to what is in front of you, rather than focusing on the future or the past. It is in the present moment that we are empowered to evolve our consciousness and our authentic presence.

STRATEGY THREE. Find Solitude.

Find a way to spend time alone with yourself to attend to the voice within. This is especially important if you feel pulled in several directions by others. Daily centering—either by spending time in nature or simply sitting still—will help to ensure that any agreements to which you commit will be aligned with your authentic self.

STRATEGY FOUR. Seek Clarity.

Make time to live your core values on a regular basis. Once you have determined your top half-dozen core values, be sure that each one of them gets scheduled into your day-planner at least once a week. If you value spirituality, for example, make room for your spiritual practice. If you value health, schedule time for regular exercise and adequate rest. If you truly value the important people in your life, spend time with them. Taking the time to find clarity about your values and priorities enables you to fulfill the most important accountability of all: accountability to *yourself.*

STRATEGY FIVE. Discover A Higher Purpose.

Focus on developing a sense of higher purpose, a vision that inspires you to be more of who you are. You are more likely to be accountable (and thus reap the rewards of greater self-respect) in those moments when the pull to do what's *easy* seems stronger than the commitment to do what's *right*, if you are working for a higher purpose beyond the impulse of comfort. This higher purpose will lift your spirits in moments of discouragement, and help you to remember that life is meant to be more than mere existence and survival. It can restore perspective and inspire you to move forward despite temptations and setbacks to lure you off course.

STRATEGY SIX. Commit To Service.

Seek ways to help lessen the burdens of others, from the cashier at the grocery store to your colleague at work. Become a contributor, a person who builds up and brings value to others, rather than just a consumer, a person who only takes. Find one social cause to which you can commit, and invest your time and energy into it.

STRATEGY SEVEN. Foster Community.

As discussed throughout this book, create a circle of authentic and account-able people in your life, people who care about you and who are committed to holding you accountable for being true to yourself. If you want to take your life or your work to a new level, it's much easier and more effective to do it with the support of others who are also committed to living accountable lives. Set goals for yourself and seek out mentors and supportive people on whom you can rely, who have qualities you admire and wish to emulate, and who will hold you to your promises.

STRATEGY EIGHT. Maintain Gratitude.

Practicing gratitude in everything you do will help sustain your accountable mindset and protect you from the poison of entitlement, blame, and victim-ization. No matter what your circumstances, reasons to be grateful are always there.

It has been said that a person who does not stand firmly for something will eventually stand for nothing. This can be said about individuals, organi-zations and perhaps about society as a whole. We hope you have discovered that accountability is much more than simply the accomplishment of tasks and results. It's not about blame or increased punishment. It is a philosophy for living and an actual force that enables you to stand firmly for something, thus enabling greatness within you and around you.

The purpose of life is to evolve and grow, both individually and collec-tively.

Authentic accountability requires a commitment to evolve consciously, and a willingness to examine the areas of your life that need changing. It is a rigorous path, but one which will ultimately enable you to become fully aligned with your authentic self and live in accordance with your deepest and truest values. And when you are fulfilled, you become a channel to inspire others to follow suit. In every situation where you can live accountably, even down to the most seemingly minor interactions, you are, in fact, helping to heal the world. Authentic accountability is the foundation of engaged and life-giving workplaces, communities, and families, and the basis of a meaningful, fulfilled, and significant life, a life of greatness. We wish you all the best on this vitally important journey.

REFERENCES

Depree, Max, *Leadership Jazz: The Art Of Conducting Business Through Leadership, Followship, Teamwork, Touch, And Voice.* New York, NY: Bantam Doubleday Dell Publishing Group, 1992.

Frankl, Victor E., *Man's Search for Meaning.* New York, NY: Washington Square Press, Simon and Schuster, 1963. First edition, 1946; revised edition, 2006.

Hummel, Charles E., *The Tyranny of the Urgent.* Downers Grove, IL: Intervarsity Press. First edition, 1967; revised edition, 1994.

Irvine, David and Jim Reger, *The Authentic Leader: It's About PRESENCE, Not Position.* Sanford, FL: DC Press, 2006.

Irvine, David. *Becoming Real: Journey to Authenticity.* Sanford, FL: DC Press. First edition, 2003; revised edition, 2007.

Irvine, David, *Simple Living in a Complex World: Balancing Life's Achievements.* Toronto, ON: Wiley & Sons, Canada, second edition, 2004.

Klatt, Bruce and Shaun Murphy, *Aligned like a Laser: Achieving Organizational Alignment Through Clear Accountabilities for Results.* Calgary, AB, Canada: Bow River Press, 2004.

Klatt, Bruce, Shaun Murphy, and David Irvine, *Accountability: Getting a Grip on Results.* Calgary, AB, Canada: Bow River Press, 2004.

Kofman, Fred, *Conscious Business: How to Build Value Through Values.* Boulder, CO: Sounds True Publication, 2006.

Popov, Linda Kavelin, with Dan Popov and John Kavelin, *The Family Virtues Guide: Simple Ways To Bring Out The Best In Our Children and Ourselves*, New York, NY: A Plume Book, 1997.

Zukav, Gary, *The Seat Of The Soul*. New York, NY: Simon & Schuster Publishers, 1989.

THE AUTHORS

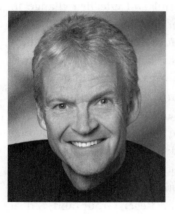

David Irvine is sought after internationally as a speaker, author, and mentor. His work has contributed to the building of accountable, vital, and engaged organizations across North America. He is the co-founder of the Newport Institute for Authentic Living whose focus is to build authentic organizational cultures that attract, retain, and unleash greatness.

David is the best-selling author of four books, with more than a quarter million copies sold worldwide: *Accountability: Getting A Grip On Results*; *The Authentic Leader: It's About PRESENCE, Not Position* (co-authored with Jim Reger); *Becoming Real: Journey To Authenticity*; and *Simple Living In A Complex World: A Guide To Balancing Life's Achievements*.

David has advanced degrees in human development, science, and social work. With more than 25 years of experience as a psychotherapist, workshop facilitator, dynamic professional speaker, and executive coach, David has developed a unique, personal and practical approach to transforming leaders. Every year, thousands of people attend David's inspiring and thought-provoking presentations and programs on authentic leadership, accountability, and balanced living.

David Irvine has dedicated his life to building great cultures through accountable and authentic leadership: inspiring, mobilizing, and guiding leaders—in all walks of life—to find their true voice. He consults with and presents to a wide range of organizations, professional associations, government, education, and health care. David has taught courses at three universities and the Banff School of Management.

To contact David, or obtain information about his books and products, keynote presentations, workshops, and coaching and consulting services:

Phone: Toll Free: (866) 621-7008
Email: david@davidirvine.com
Web site: www.davidirvine.com

Jim Reger's passion and commitment for facilitating powerful and effective change in individuals and organizations is evident in his work, which is focused on assisting leaders in creating and building authentic lives and cultures in their organizations, families and communities. Jim is an internationally experienced speaker and leadership mentor with a unique and varied background—including more than 25 years in the information industry, both in senior executive positions with large multi-nationals as well as a number of technology start-ups. Jim is the founder of The Reger Group and Global Learning Opportunities, which are learning organizations focused on providing the key leadership skills required for success in business and in life. More than 2,000 individuals across Canada have graduated from their extensive entrepreneurial development programs.

Across North America and Australia thousands of business owners and executives have attended Jim's inspiring and thought-provoking presentations on *The Authentic Leader; Creating a Shared Vision;* and *Living a Life of Meaning and Significance.*

The Reger Group is a family business and Jim and his daughter Natasha work extensively with business families addressing the special challenges they face as they move through their life cycles and struggle with the unique effects that family dynamics have on their businesses and their lives. As